Handwriting
Research and Resources

A Guide to Curriculum Planning

Zaner-Bloser

Acknowledgments

"We Still Need to Teach and Value Handwriting" reprinted from *Literacy at the Crossroads: Crucial Talk About Reading, Writing, and Other Teaching Dilemmas* by Regie Routman. Copyright © 1996 by Regie Routman. Published by Heinemann, a division of Reed Elsevier Inc., Portsmouth, NH. Used by permission of the publisher.

Excerpt from "Handwriting: A Neglected Cornerstone of Literacy" reprinted from *Annals of Dyslexia*, Vol. 46, 1996, by Betty Sheffield, with Permission of The International Dyslexia Association, July 28, 2000.

"Research-Based Findings on Handwriting" © Harford County Public Schools Office of Curriculum and Instruction, Bel Air, MD.

"Handwriting in an Early Childhood Curriculum" by Linda Leonard Lamme is a major revision of an article that first appeared in *Young Children*, Vol. 35, No. 1, (Nov., 1979), 20–27.

Excerpt from *Beginning to Read: Thinking and Learning About Print* by Marilyn Jager Adams, © 1990 Massachusetts Institute of Technology, published by The MIT Press. Reprinted by permission.

"The Effect of Handwriting Style on Alphabet Recognition" by Debby Kuhl and Peter Dewitz. Paper presented at the Annual Meeting of the American Educational Research Association, April 1, 1994, New Orleans, LA. Reprinted by permission.

"Are Slanted Manuscript Alphabets Superior to the Traditional Manuscript Alphabet?" by Steve Graham (1993/94) *Childhood Education*, 70, 91–95. Reprinted by permission of Steve Graham and the Association for Childhood Education International, 17904 Georgia Avenue, Suite 215, Olney, MD 20832. Copyright © 1993/94 by the Association.

Excerpt from "Handwriting Instruction" from *Introduction to Teaching the Language Arts, 1st edition*, by E.P. Ross © 1990. Reprinted with permission of Wadsworth, an imprint of the Wadsworth Group, a division of Thomson Learning. Fax 800 730-2215.

Excerpt from "Handwriting: A Communication Tool" © 1992 Saskatchewan Education. From *English Language Arts: A Curriculum Guide for the Elementary Level*. Regina, SK: Saskatchewan Education.

"A Rub-Out? Why the Pencil Will Survive" by Henry Petroski, *The New Republic*, December 6, 1993. Reprinted by permission of *The New Republic*, © 1993, The New Republic, Inc.

"They Can't Write!" by Edward E. Ericson, Jr., *American Enterprise Institute for Public Policy Research*, Sept./Oct., 1996, Vol. 7, No. 5.

"Handwriting Goes With the Flow" by Stephen Lee, Copyrighted April 9, 1996, Chicago Tribune Company. All rights reserved. Used with permission.

"Schools Promote Handwritten Letters," *Siuslaw News*, Florence, Oregon, May 10, 2000. Reprinted by permission.

"D'Nealian and Zaner-Bloser Manuscript Alphabets and Initial Transition to Cursive Handwriting," *Journal of Educational Research*, Vol. 77, No. 6, July/Aug., 1984. Reprinted by permission of Louis J. LaNunziata, Aug. 30, 2000.

"Handwriting Instruction: Key to Good Writing" by Cheryl Murfin Bond. *Seattle's Child & Eastside Parent,* Oct., 1998. Reprinted by permission of the author.

Excerpts from "Is Handwriting Causally Related to Learning to Write? Treatment of Handwriting Problems in Beginning Writers" by Steve Graham, Karen R. Harris, and Barbara Fink, in-press, *Journal of Educational Psychology.* Copyright © 2001 by the American Psychological Association. Reprinted with permission.

Excerpts from "Relationship Between Automaticity in Handwriting and Students' Ability to Generate Written Text" by Dian Jones and Carol A. Christensen, *Journal of Educational Psychology,* Vol. 91, No. 1, 44–49. Copyright © 1999 by the American Psychological Association. Reprinted with permission.

"Technology and the Oops! Effect: Finding a Bias Against Word Processing" by M.D. Roblyer, *Learning and Leading With Technology,* Vol. 24. Copyright © 1997 by International Society for Technology in Education. Reproduced with permission of International Society for Technology in Education via Copyright Clearance Center.

"What Is Excellent Writing?" by Jim Henry. From *Instructor,* September 1995. Copyright © 1995 by Scholastic Inc. Reprinted by permission of Scholastic Inc.

"Helpful Handwriting Hints" by Lisa A. Kurtz from *Teaching Exceptional Children,* Vol. 27, 1994, 58–59. Copyright © 1994 by The Council for Exceptional Children. Reprinted with permission.

"Helping Hands: A World of Manipulatives to Boost Handwriting Skills" by June M. Naus from *Teaching Exceptional Children,* Vol. 32, 2000, 64–70. Copyright © 2000 by The Council for Exceptional Children. Reprinted with permission.

ISBN   0-7367-0391-8

Copyright © Zaner-Bloser, Inc.

Zaner-Bloser, Inc., P.O. Box 16764, Columbus, Ohio 43216-6764 (1-800-421-3018)

www.zaner-bloser.com

Printed in the United States of America

05 06 07 (415) 8 7

Contents

Contents

REAL LIFE ADVENTURES

The computer generation.

Preface

Steve Graham
Professor and Distinguished Scholar Teacher
University of Maryland
School of Education

After being introduced as a very good writer, Harold Pinter was approached by a six-year-old who asked the famous playwright if he could write the letter **w**. I suspect that the child's own difficulties with this letter prompted his question, and that he judged the writing capabilities of others accordingly. Such judgments are not uncommon, especially in schools, where the grades that teachers assign are influenced not only by a paper's content, but by the quality of the students' penmanship as well. When teachers or other adults are asked to grade multiple versions of the same paper, differing only in handwriting quality, more neatly written papers receive higher marks for writing content than papers that are less legible.

Another consequence of poor penmanship is captured in the following childhood joke:

> "Can you do anything that other people can't?"
> "Sure, I can read my own handwriting."

For children and adults, communication is compromised whenever part or all of the text is illegible. The impact of illegible handwriting extends well beyond missed communications, however, creating problems that range from undelivered tax refunds to life-threatening errors for patients receiving medical services.

Handwriting also plays a critical role in writing development. One way of illustrating its impact on writing is to imagine that you have been asked to write something using a Chinese typewriter. This is the most complicated typewriter in the world, containing 5,850 characters. As you search for the characters needed to produce the next word in your masterpiece, some of the ideas and writing plans you are trying to hold in memory will undoubtedly be lost, as most of your attention is consumed by trying to transcribe words into print. It will also be difficult to create additional plans or sharpen intentions for the segment of text you are currently producing, as most of your attention is directed at locating the next character to be typed. Even if you are an expert with a Chinese typewriter, flying along at an incredible speed of 11 words a minute, your typing will still be too slow to keep up with your thoughts.

Although most of us will never experience the "joy" of using a Chinese typewriter, we have at one time or another experienced similar frustrations from our own limited handwriting skills. Most likely, this involved the loss of a good idea that irrevocably slipped from memory because we were unable to write all of our thoughts down fast enough. For children, however, handwriting can be so "taxing" that it influences the pace and course of their writing development. For example, the physical act of handwriting is so strenuous for many beginning writers that they develop an approach to writing that minimizes the use of other composing processes, such as planning, because these processes are also mentally demanding. Just as importantly, children who experience difficulty mastering handwriting often avoid writing and develop a mind-set that they cannot write, leading to arrested writing development.

Finally, poor handwriting is the thief of one of our most valuable commodities—time. Teachers lose precious time, often time that they cannot spare, trying to decipher papers that are illegible. On the other hand, the handwriting of some children is so slow that it takes them almost twice as long to produce the same text as their more facile class-mates, exerting a heavy toll on their productivity. These same children find it difficult to keep pace when taking notes during class.

Despite the importance of handwriting to school success, writing development, and written communication, the teaching of handwriting has been de-emphasized in some schools in recent years. Although handwriting continues to be taught in most classrooms nationwide, it is taught sporadically, if at all, in others. In these classrooms, it is often assumed that handwriting will develop naturally, by immersing children in a literacy-rich environment where they have plenty of opportunities to write and read for real purposes. While this assumption has a com-forting simplicity, absolving schools from the responsibility of directly teaching handwriting, there is no scientific evidence to support it. In contrast, there is almost a century of research that demonstrates the power of directly and systematically teaching handwriting.

A personal analogy may help to illustrate the folly of the "natural" approach to handwriting development. I learned to type when I first started to use the word processor at work. Along the way, I developed some bad habits, such as having to look at the keyboard and using just three or four fingers to type. Unfortunately, these habits act like a hobble, limiting the speed of my typing. As I learned too late, discovery is not an especially effective approach for learning either typing or handwriting.

Another argument that is sometimes used as a justification for not teaching handwriting is that it is obsolete. For years, I have heard rumors about the demise of handwriting, as it would soon be replaced by word processing or speech synthesis (prior to that it was the typewriter). While these tools have clearly become a more prominent part of everyday life, handwriting has not been superseded. Much writing is still done by hand, especially in schools, and barring a major change in school funding, this is unlikely to change anytime in the near future.

Hopefully, I have convinced you that handwriting is important and that schools should be in the business of systematically teaching this skill to children. The articles reprinted in this book reinforce and extend these points:

- **Chapter 1** examines why handwriting should be taught and valued. It also provides a concise summary of research-based findings on handwriting and its instruction.

- **Chapter 2** addresses one of the most contentious issues in handwriting today; namely, the type of script that should be used in beginning handwriting instruction. The material in this section supports the teaching of vertical manuscript to young children in kindergarten and the early primary grades.

- **Chapter 3** provides critical recommendations on teaching handwriting, emphasizing basic skills such as how to sit, hold the writing instrument, and position the paper.

- **Chapter 4** argues that children should be taught cursive in addition to manuscript and examines the transition between the two types of script.

- **Chapter 5** explores the connections between handwriting and good writing, showing that accurate and fluent handwriting is an essential ingredient in the writing development of young children.

- **Chapter 6** presents practical information and advice on a frequently overlooked aspect of handwriting instruction—assessment. This includes making handwriting assessment part of students' portfolios.

- **Chapter 7** focuses on individual differences in handwriting and explains what teachers can do to help all children develop good handwriting.

Taken together, these materials provide an excellent summary of what we know about handwriting today.

Chapter 1

Why is it important to teach handwriting?

Reprinted with permission. Ford Button, deceased.

Introduction

Why teach handwriting? It's a skill that may seem old-fashioned, requiring only pencil, paper, and chalkboard. Today's language arts curriculum is crowded, and our expectations for the literacy skills we want students to learn are higher than ever before. Internet skills, reading goals, and state testing all compete for instructional time. Is it still necessary to teach handwriting? Can it be eliminated from a teacher's already-busy day?

The answer to these questions is that handwriting is important. Like spelling, grammar, and phonics, handwriting is a support skill that helps build a strong foundation for student success. Failure to teach and value good handwriting can have far-reaching consequences. As the articles in this chapter show, educators and researchers are reaffirming some old reasons, and discovering some new reasons, to teach handwriting. Consider these points:

Students still need to know how to write by hand.

Although many students today have ample access to computers, there seem to be more occasions than ever when handwriting is required. For commenting on a partner's paper, copying an assignment from the board, or jotting an important fact from a book or Web site, there is no replacement for the speed and convenience of writing by hand. Until budgets allow a computer on every desk, handwriting will continue to be the principal means of communication at school.

Good handwriting makes a good impression.

Parents are pleased to see neat, legible writing on a spelling paper. Community visitors admire nicely handwritten stories displayed in a school hallway. Test evaluators take notice of the way good handwriting tends to accompany complete, well-written essays. In these and many other ways, valuing legible handwriting helps to set a high standard for student achievement.

Teaching handwriting boosts writing proficiency.

A child who has internalized the rules for good spelling, grammar, and handwriting has a big advantage when it comes time to write a story or essay. He or she can devote more concentration to the content of the writing and the way ideas are expressed. Before legible

Why is it important to teach handwriting?

handwriting becomes automatic, children must spend a lot of their composing time thinking about how to form letters.

Illegible writing wastes time and money.

It's not difficult to find examples of the costs of messy writing in the adult world. The U.S. Postal Service spends millions of dollars each year to decipher scrawled addresses. Illegible prescriptions can endanger patients' lives. At school, the effects of careless handwriting may be less dramatic, but they are significant. Time is wasted when teachers can't read papers and when students can't read their own notes and drafts.

Teaching and valuing good handwriting does take the commitment of teachers and administrators, but it doesn't take a lot of time. Handwriting is best taught in short, frequent periods of direct instruction. Fifteen minutes a day, several times a week, is enough. After watching their teachers model good letter formation, students need to practice writing legibly. Handwriting must be taught; it can't be "caught" in the context of other language arts skills.

The articles in this chapter make convincing arguments for taking time to teach handwriting. Regie Routman discusses the special, personal quality of students' handwritten work. Betty Sheffield states that children appreciate being taught how to write carefully and consistently. Finally, a document from the Harford County Public Schools in Bel Air, Maryland, presents twenty-five useful, research-based findings about handwriting.

We Still Need to Teach and Value Handwriting

Regie Routman

*When we teach and value handwriting, we are sending
a message to students and parents that we value legibility,
attention to detail, neatness, correctness, and excellence.*

Handwriting can be an emotionally charged issue. In the language arts support group in one of my district's elementary buildings, we spent several weeks talking about expectations for handwriting. Lots of issues surfaced. Should we teach lowercase letters in kindergarten? Are we asking children to write too much too soon? Is legibility enough? How much time should we spend teaching stroke formation? When should we begin teaching cursive? How much practice and repetition is necessary? Because the research on teaching handwriting is scarce and conflicting, we had difficulty resolving these issues. Nonetheless, most of us were able to agree that handwriting is important to us and to many of our students' parents and that legibility is the desired goal.

When we teach and value handwriting, we are sending a message to students and parents that we value legibility, attention to detail, neatness, correctness, and excellence. To write beautifully by hand takes time, practice, and pride. It is literally a dying art. I welcome a handwritten letter. It seems to be more personal and to have more voice than a word-processed one. I love to get "h-mail—handwritten and heartwritten." I save all personal, handwritten letters and cards in a special file for future reference and rereading. (By contrast, I am much less likely to save a letter received through e-mail.) When I want to send a personal message, I always handwrite it on special paper or beautiful blank cards.

Yes, we can print out computer-generated, spell-checked material, and this is great much of the time. Indeed, for some students, word-processing has freed up the process of writing, and that has been terrific. We need to remember, though, that just because a finished piece looks professional doesn't mean that it's better written or even well written. For me, these printed pieces can lack the voice and personal style that comes through in a handwritten piece.

Why is it important to teach handwriting?

Let me give you an example. At the end of the school year, fourth-grade teacher Joan Servis and I worked with her students to write final-evaluation narratives. These "report cards," written by the students, were not supplementary to the teacher's report; they were the official reports.... The students went through drafts and revisions and took the project very seriously. Almost all final reports were word-processed so they would look professional. They were so well crafted, complete, and official-looking that it "looked" as if the students couldn't possibly have done them. In retrospect, Joan and I noticed that the narratives of the few late finishers, who handwrote their final reports, stood out for their uniqueness. The individual handwriting styles made those narratives look child-centered and personal. This year we are going to have all students handwrite their final narratives.

Or again, third-grade teacher Danny Young—who does a marvelous job with writing workshop—found out that his kids couldn't handwrite very well when they needed to. While his students were publishing pieces of excellent quality, everything that went to final copy was word-processed on the computer. When Danny

> **Because the book reviews of their favorite books were going to be displayed at the local book store, the handwriting had to be polished and legible.**

and I, working together, taught the students how to write book reviews, we found out that their handwriting was sorely lacking. Because the book reviews of their favorite books were going to be displayed at the local book store, the handwriting had to be polished and legible. Therefore, Danny took the time—in a meaningful context and for a mutually valued purpose (not as a copying exercise)—to teach handwriting and to revalue it.

What We Can Do About Handwriting
Educate parents about the importance of early play in the home.

While the research on handwriting is conflicting, one thing is certain. We are seeing more kids who have difficulty with handwriting because they haven't had enough motor experience with their hands. Instead of manipulating and playing with blocks, they have been sedentary—spending excessive time in front of the television.

Make sure parents know we teach handwriting.

Parents, used to the importance of handwriting from their own schooling, expect handwriting to be taught. Use journals or daily writing to diagnose and observe penmanship. Formally teach stroke formation in the lower grades, and give time for practice. Make the goal legibility.

Make sure parents know we value handwriting.

Do mention handwriting in newsletters; post handwritten work; expect students to handwrite some final copies—personal letters, for example. Let parents know we value and expect legibility and quality penmanship.

By permission of Johnny Hart and Creators Syndicate, Inc.

Why is it important to teach handwriting?

An Excerpt From

Handwriting: A Neglected Cornerstone of Literacy

Betty Sheffield

*It is argued here that automatic legible writing is an essential basis
for written expression. And yet, crowded school curricula and neglect
by educational institutions and researchers often leave no room
for appropriate and sufficient attention to teaching this critical skill.
This is unfortunate because early consistent teaching
of handwriting is crucial to success in school.*

As with so much else in American education, the perceived importance of teaching accurate handwriting goes in cycles. Berninger (1994)
comments on "the zebra syndrome, with its either/or logic" in philoso-
phy of teaching. She criticizes education's tendency to focus on what is
stylish at the moment rather than incorporating a more global approach
to training teachers and teaching students. Phelps and Stempel (1987)
speak of the "shifting emphasis away from the teaching of handwriting...during the sixties," with penmanship back again in style at the
time of their article. Now that whole language is often the teaching
method of choice, the American school system is working its way
through another wave of handwriting not being taught directly.

It is argued here that automatic legible writing is an essential basis
for written expression. And yet, crowded school curricula and neglect by
educational institutions and researchers often leave no room for appropriate and sufficient attention to teaching this critical skill. This is
unfortunate because early consistent teaching of handwriting is crucial
to success in school. Decisions about what to teach, how to teach, and
when to teach handwriting need to be based on what is essential for
children rather than on accepted custom, current fad, or inadequate
research.

Importance of Direct Early Teaching of Handwriting

There are at least three reasons handwriting must be carefully taught
to all children. First, handwriting allows access to kinesthetic memory,
our earliest, strongest, and most reliable memory channel. Second,
serviceable handwriting needs to be at a spontaneous level so that a

student is free to concentrate on spelling, and to focus on higher-level thought and written expression. Third, teachers judge and grade students based on the appearance of their work, and the world judges adults on the quality of their handwriting.

Handwriting is important because it taps into kinesthetic learning. Our first and strongest memory system is the kinesthetic one (Zaporozhets and Elkonin 1971). Competent writing is our access to utilization of this crucial channel for school learning. Because kinesthetic learning is such a strong learning channel and so reliable, all children need to assimilate accurate formation of alphabet letters to a point that forming these letters requires no conscious effort. Dyslexic students in particular often need to use writing in order to learn to read. All students have a right to comfortable, legible, and automatic handwriting.

Handwriting provides an essential basis for higher-level written work. Competent handwriting frees a student to concentrate on a higher level of written content. Vail speaks of the "paralytic cumulative effects of handwriting problems" (Vail 1986). At an early age, a child must memorize the names, shapes, and orientation of letters, a task made more difficult by a lack of direct teaching.

> All students have a right to comfortable, legible, and automatic handwriting. Handwriting provides an essential basis for higher-level written work.

Emphasizing how often this automaticity is not achieved, Phelps, Stempel, and Speck (1985) studied 1372 Dallas students in grades 3 through 8. They concluded that 10% of the 3rd and 4th graders had difficulty with speed and legibility. And 20% of the 5th through 8th graders tested wrote too slowly to meet school demands. Many high school students cannot write legibly or quickly enough to deal with their school work.

Handwriting is often a criterion used to judge a person's intelligence or level of education. Students and adults with poor handwriting are judged and judge themselves on their handwriting. In Great Britain, Briggs (1970) researched the effect of poor handwriting on the grading of 6th grade essays. Ten comparable essays on the subject of "the day of the big fog" were chosen from the work of 100 children. The essays were copied in a variety of excellent to terrible handwriting styles. The essays were then judged by ten different groups of teachers from ten different schools. The quality of handwriting did affect grading by experienced markers regardless of the papers' content. Alston and Taylor (1987) report on research conducted by Briggs in 1980 in which already graded exams by college seniors were copied in different handwriting styles. These copies were then graded by experienced graders. There was significant variation in grading based on the quality of handwriting. Alston and Taylor (1987) add that "problems in this mechanical skill are likely to spill over into the child's level of success and failure throughout the curriculum."

Reasons for Insufficient Attention Being Paid to Handwriting

Lack of Research

One difficulty in dealing with the subject of teaching handwriting is the scant amount of useful published research. Phelps and Stempel (1989) characterize this field of study as developing rapidly but still poorly researched. Alston and Taylor (1987) have surveyed the teaching of handwriting in the United Kingdom and to some extent in America. They speak of "fashions in teaching that...have considerable influence...despite the fact that there is little empirical foundation for their promotion." Peck, Askov, and Fairchild (1980), in their survey of research in handwriting, mention a lack of research concerning production and legibility of writing. They also complain of the lack of statistical studies measuring the value of manuscript versus cursive writing for initial teaching of primary children with specific learning disabilities.

Lack of Preparation of Teachers

Phelps and Stempel (1989) believe that many teachers in the early grades pay little attention to handwriting because they themselves have been given little training in methods of teaching it. Many elementary teachers assume that handwriting is a skill that children learn informally, that handwriting will come easily and by osmosis, and that children will be bored by the repetition necessary for acquiring a reliable skill. They cannot look into the future and foresee some 8th grade teacher faced with poorly prepared students who write illegibly and slowly. Teachers often lack the understanding that handwriting is a skill that demands "a competent level of instruction" (Alston and Taylor 1987). They seem unaware that children will practice to achieve mastery when they can see positive results.

Classroom teachers may not be aware of the long-term benefits of careful consistent teaching of handwriting. The curricula in our schools are so packed with requirements that it is often difficult to include the basics. Although the time required for teaching handwriting is not so great, it has to be incorporated regularly into a class schedule. Novice teachers, if they teach the mechanics of writing at all, are often thrown upon the resource of using publishers' copybooks. They expect children to copy, self-teach, and internalize the material. And yet, without direct teaching, the attempt to learn writing often ends in disaster. Any 1st grade child can find and lock onto endless inefficient ways of scribbling around the same letter. Many cases of apparent dysgraphia are the result of inadequate teaching.

> Classroom teachers may not be aware of the long-term benefits of careful consistent teaching of handwriting.

Teachers should not be blamed for their lack of preparation. The inadequate attention paid to handwriting appears to be based on a lack of emphasis at the level of state and local school system guidelines. Nolen, McCutchen, and Berninger (1990) state, "The responsibility for the nation's literacy...belongs not to the classroom teacher alone, but also to the institutions that educate teachers and the states that certify them." These authors conducted a survey of state certification requirements in teaching reading and writing. They received replies from forty-eight out of fifty states. Twenty-nine states required coursework in reading for elementary certification. The data received on writing was not definitive. Only eight states reported writing coursework requirements. There was no apparent mention of handwriting, although handwriting might have been included under the general term of Language Arts. In a brief discussion of Public Law 94-142, the authors allude to the fact that the law suggests no means by which classroom teachers could update their information about writing disorders, and that local schools often implement any reeducation in brief inadequate workshops (Nolen, McCutchen, and Berninger 1990).

American schools are not alone in their neglect of handwriting. According to Alston and Taylor (1987), there is also inconsistency in the teaching of handwriting in British schools. "In the absence of educational guidelines, freedom of what or how one will teach is left to the individual school staff or even to the individual teacher."

In the late 1960s, I taught at a private school that prided itself on its creative and gifted children. The school boasted a long-held belief that emphasis on handwriting would destroy a child's freedom of expression. The school's collective handwriting was atrocious. Spelling was worse. As a neophyte remedial specialist, I needed to identify 1st and 2nd grade children in need of extra help. I administered the Slingerland Screening tests to all our children at the beginning of the 1st and 2nd grades (Slingerland 1969). Roughly half of the 2nd graders were conspicuously identifiable as in trouble with reversals, inversions, and confusions. Standardized tests revealed levels of reading and spelling that were below expectation.

When a new principal arrived at the school, he took one horrified look at the children's work and told the remedial department to oversee the *correct* teaching of handwriting. As an initial step, the 1st, 2nd, and 3rd grade teachers compared the handwriting forms each was using. It was hard to believe that one small school could incorporate so many different patterns for the same letters. A child, moving from one grade to another, was confronted every year with an entirely new set of letter forms. Faced with that unexpected discovery, the teachers came to a consensus on how each letter should be consistently written. They agreed to teach these letter forms directly instead of turning unsupervised children loose with individual writing books.

> First and 2nd graders loved being taught how to do an accurate job.

The children were ecstatic! First and 2nd graders loved being taught how to do an accurate job. Teachers quickly learned that when they were writing on the board, they had to display extra care. If an l or a k was slightly off vertical, a chorus of happy young voices would chide, "Teacher! Remember! No leaning towers!" Youngsters at that level wanted to be shown what was *correct*. They did not mind practicing because they desired to be successful and to produce. They did not resent structure—they welcomed it.

A year later there was a dramatic change in Slingerland screening scores. The number of 2nd, 3rd, and 4th graders having difficulty with written language was significantly lower. The school was no longer turning so many borderline children into problems.

References

Alston, J., and Taylor, J. 1987. *Handwriting: Theory, Research and Practice.* London & Sydney: Croom Helm.

Berninger, V. W. 1994. *Reading and Writing Acquisition: A Developmental Neuropsychological Perspective.* Madison, WI: Brown & Benchmark.

Briggs, D. 1970. The influence of handwriting on assessment. *Educational Research* 13(1): 50-55.

Nolen, P., McCutchen, D., and Berninger, B. 1990. Ensuring tomorrow's literacy: A shared responsibility. *Journal of Teacher Education* 41: 63-72.

Peck, M., Askov, E., and Fairchild, S. 1980. Another decade of research in handwriting: Progress and prospect in the 1970s. *Journal of Educational Research* 89: 283-98.

Phelps, J., Stempel, L., and Speck, G. 1985. The children's handwriting scale: A new diagnostic tool. *Journal of Educational Research* 79: 46-50.

Phelps, J., and Stempel, L. 1987. Handwriting: Evolution and evaluation. *Annals of Dyslexia* 37: 228-39.

Phelps, J., and Stempel, L. 1989. Help for handwriting: Procedures developed at Scottish Rite Hospital. *Education* 109(4): 388-89.

Slingerland, B. H. 1969. *Slingerland Screening Tests for Identifying Children with Specific Language Disability.* Cambridge, MA: Educators Publishing Service.

Vail, P. 1986. By hand with ergs and ohms. *Newsletter of the New York Branch of the International Orton Dyslexia Society* 10(2): 1.

Zaporozhets, A., and Elkonin, D. 1971. *Psychology of Preschool Children.* Cambridge, MA: MIT Press.

Research-Based Findings on Handwriting

Harford County Public Schools, Bel Air, MD

It is important that teachers recognize the importance of intentional teaching of handwriting skills throughout the elementary years.

The following findings are based on careful review of the research and should be considered in every handwriting program:

1. The principal objective of handwriting instruction is to help each student learn to write legibly.

2. Handwriting is a basic communication skill that is used early in the school life of a student. To facilitate communication, it is imperative that students write legibly with ease and fluency.

3. Emphasis in recent years on writing as a process, rather than a product, has influenced the instruction of handwriting as a tool of writing.

4. The increased use of word processors has resulted in fewer handwritten assignments and poorer legibility overall.

5. The quality of a student's handwriting can influence raters' judgment of the quality of content of compositions (Marshall & Powers, 1969).

6. It is important that teachers recognize the importance of intentional teaching of handwriting skills throughout the elementary years.

7. Language arts methods texts largely support the formal, rather than informal, instruction of handwriting.

8. It cannot be assumed that children will develop proper handwriting skills informally. Children need to be taught the basic aspects of handwriting, or they will learn improper techniques.

9. Teachers in early childhood education should teach handwriting through direct instruction for it is a basic and important skill for writing.

10. Two things are critical in handwriting teaching strategies: (1) children should be taught handwriting and (2) they should practice

the handwriting skills taught (Ellis, Standal, Pennau & Rummell, 1989, p. 244).

11. What appears to be important in the development of handwriting is the amount of emphasis teachers place on legible, neat writing, and also the presence in the classroom of good handwriting models (Koenke, 1986, Milone & Wasylyk, 1981).

12. According to Hoskisson & Tompkins (1987), "Handwriting is best taught in separate periods of direct instruction (isolation) and teacher supervised practice. As soon as skills are taught, they are applied in real-life writing activities within the classroom (integration)" (p. 444).

13. Handwriting may be evaluated informally by the teacher and the pupil or formally through the use of a published scale. Evaluations should lead to remedial teaching and corrective practices.

14. Legibility (well proportioned, uniformly arranged letters and words) and fluency (rate of writing) are critical criteria in determining handwriting quality.

15. Readiness in handwriting is just as important as readiness in reading or other subjects. Muscle development, eye-hand coordination, and visual discrimination are important. Teachers need to be sensitive to the developmental needs of students experiencing difficulties in these areas.

16. Summaries of current practices indicate that handwriting instruction is fairly uniform throughout the United States. It is typical to begin manuscript writing in the first grade with a transition to cursive writing sometime before the third grade.

17. The time of transition is not as important as the nature of the instructional program.

18. Students who are left handed face unusual circumstances in learning to write because the basic instruction is oriented to the majority who are right handed. Natural-handedness should be determined before students begin to learn to write. If a student has strong left handed tendencies, he/she should be taught to write with the left hand.

19. Research has shown that the number of students who rely solely upon manuscript handwriting is increasing with approximately 1 out of every 26 students using only manuscript handwriting. For

Why is it important to teach handwriting?

some of these students their cursive is totally illegible. There is a need for instruction in both manuscript and cursive, and a balance in their use in grades four and five.

20. The preferred form of writing, cursive or manuscript, in higher grades has generated considerable debate. Evidence is sparse to show that cursive is faster to write or more legible to read. Hence, both writing forms should be maintained. Students should be free, at times, to use the form with which they are more comfortable, and capable enough to use either as required by the teacher.

21. Poor handwriting costs American business and taxpayers $200 million a year.

22. Hundreds of thousands of tax returns are delayed every year because of illegible handwriting. Sloppily written addresses and other mistakes can delay income tax refunds for 3-4 weeks.

23. An illegibly written barometer reading is blamed for a plane crash that killed 5 people.

24. Nearly 20% of hospital medicine orders are returned by pharmacists as illegible.

25. 38 million illegibly addressed letters cost the U.S. Postal Service $4 million a year.

References

_____. (1992) *American Demographics*. Dec.

_____. (1989) *Better Handwriting in Thirty Days*.

Ellis, A., Standal, T., Pennau, T., & Rummell, M. K. (1989) *Elementary Language Arts*. Englewood Cliffs, N.J.: Prentice Hall.

Hoskisson, K., & Tompkins, G. E. (1987) *Language Arts: Content and Teaching Strategies*. Columbus, OH: Merrill.

Koenke, K. (1986) "Handwriting Instruction: What Do We Know?" *The Reading Teacher*. 40, 14-16.

Kusumoto, Kay. (1993) "Penmanship Burdens the Bottom Link." *The Statesman Journal*. Nov.

Marshall, J. C., & Powers, J. M. (1969) "Writing Neatness, Composition Errors, and Essay Grades." *Journal of Educational Measurement*. 6, 72-101.

Milone, M. N. Jr., & Wasylyk, T. M. (1981) "Handwriting in Special Education." *Teaching Exceptional Children*. 14, 58-61.

Chapter 2

Vertical manuscript:
Why is it appropriate for beginning readers and writers?

By permission of Rick Detorie and Creators Syndicate, Inc.

Introduction

What is vertical manuscript and why is it a good choice for young children? Vertical manuscript is the straight-up-and-down writing style that most resembles print. Marjorie Wise and other early childhood educators introduced manuscript to American elementary schools in the 1920s. They recognized that the standard style of the time, the ornate cursive Palmer method, required a high degree of fine-motor skill and hand-eye coordination. Young children, they argued, needed a simpler, more developmentally appropriate way to write.

Today, the rounded, upright letters of the manuscript alphabet are such a familiar sight in kindergarten and first-grade classrooms that we may be tempted to think they are as old-fashioned as an apple on the teacher's desk. Primary teachers might wonder if keyboarding should replace regular handwriting instruction, or if they should adopt an italic style (such as D'Nealian) that claims to speed children ahead to cursive.

The articles in this chapter explain why learning to write the vertical manuscript alphabet plays a significant role in children's literacy development, and why it should remain a vital part of the language arts curriculum. Here are some of the most important reasons.

Vertical manuscript is familiar.

Vertical manuscript is the alphabet young children see on "Sesame Street," in picture books, and on road signs. An awareness of this environmental print leads to children's interest in letters and their shapes. Parents and preschool teachers often introduce vertical manuscript when they teach children to write their names. Slanted or italic writing is not supported by children's everyday environment.

Vertical manuscript is easy for children to write.

The basic strokes that make up the letters of Zaner-Bloser's continuous-stroke manuscript alphabet are vertical lines, horizontal lines, and circles. These simple shapes occur naturally in children's drawings, signaling readiness for handwriting instruction. By contrast, italic alphabets include small curves and "tails" that are difficult for young children to write.

Vertical manuscript is highly legible.

Just as vertical manuscript is the most legible style of type for traffic signs and job applications, it also helps make children's writing more readable to them and their teachers. It's a style that can be learned quickly and put to work right away in children's own writing.

Vertical manuscript supports early reading.

With vertical manuscript, children learn to write the same letters they see in books, strengthening the reading-writing connection. Additionally, learning to print focuses children's attention on the distinctive shapes and features of letters in a way that simply finding a letter on a keyboard cannot. Studying the shapes of letters during handwriting instruction can lead to improved letter recognition—one of the most reliable indicators of future reading success.

Vertical manuscript is a life-long skill.

Manuscript is a skill that needs to be practiced and maintained throughout the elementary and middle school years. Students will encounter the directions "Please print" throughout their lives. Many older students continue to prefer manuscript writing over cursive for the majority of classroom writing tasks.

The articles in this chapter explore the benefits of teaching manuscript to young children. First, Linda Lamme looks at the developmental needs of young writers and explains how handwriting fits into an early childhood curriculum. Second, Marilyn Jager Adams tells us how writing letters can enhance children's early reading skills. Third, a study by kindergarten classroom researchers Debby Kuhl and Peter Dewitz finds evidence that the D'Nealian alphabet can cause confusion for young readers and interfere with letter recognition. Last, Steve Graham examines the vertical and slanted manuscript styles and concludes that there is no evidence to support the use of slanted writing in the early grades.

Zaner-Bloser Continuous-Stroke Manuscript

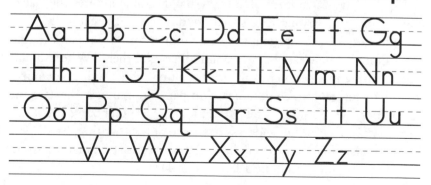

Handwriting in an Early Childhood Curriculum

Linda Leonard Lamme

During...emergence into handwriting, there are six physical and mental abilities that support the child's growth: small muscle development, eye-hand coordination, holding a writing tool, basic strokes, letter perception, and orientation to printed language.

Handwriting continues to be taught to young children today in more and more kindergarten and preschool programs. Children have long been taught to write their names (usually in uppercase letters) at home by eager parents who find them highly motivated to acquire this skill. With more and more children attending preschool at earlier ages, it may be early childhood teachers and not parents who explain and demonstrate to young children how to write their names. But to assume that children who can write their names are ready to write all letters and words may be a fallacy.

Some children are being pushed into formal handwriting instruction before they have acquired competence in emergent stages of handwriting. While children are unique in their development of the ability to handwrite, there are certain landmark experiences that most writers have that make formal handwriting instruction easier and more effective. As young children emerge from scribbling to mock writing and to alphabet letter writing, they acquire competence at using writing tools in ways that communicate on paper. When formal handwriting instruction occurs too early in their development, children become discouraged. They overcompensate for the handwriting abilities they lack, thus causing poor writing habits that are difficult to correct later.

What are the abilities that prepare children for formal handwriting instruction, and how can we help children acquire them? When should formal writing instruction begin? Studies of preschool writing demonstrate that children can communicate on paper long before they acquire the ability to write legibly (Hall, 1989; Hall, 1991; Hubbard, 1989; Olson, 1992). Few authors address the issue of handwriting, however. We know that children progress in a relatively consistent manner from scribbling to writing (Lamme 1985)(Table 1).

TABLE I. Patterns of handwriting development

level	example	description
random scribbling		• child not aware that he or she is making marks on paper • no patterns
controlled scribbling		• patterns emerge (lines of different colors; circles of different sizes)
naming scribbling		• romances while scribbling • gives names to scribbles
mock writing		• forms look like alphabet letters • manuscript and cursive forms occur
alphabet letter writing		• alphabet letters randomly placed on the page • linear alphabet letter strings with some reversals

During this emergence into handwriting, there are six physical and mental abilities that support the child's growth: small muscle development, eye-hand coordination, holding a writing tool, basic strokes, letter perception, and orientation to printed language.

Small Muscle Development

Children need small muscle coordination in order to properly hold and control a pencil or writing tool. Small muscle coordination activities are not typically considered part of a handwriting curriculum in an early childhood classroom, but they clearly are.

Activities that enhance small muscle development include many manipulative tasks. Jigsaw puzzles can be graded from easy (with a few large pieces) to complex (with many small pieces). Manipulative toys such as Legos, Tinker Toys, and snap beads are excellent for small muscle development. Play with small motor vehicles, miniature gas stations, Transformers, dollhouses, etc., gives children experience in using small muscles.

Molding opportunities are indispensable. Clay, sand, play dough, Silly Putty, real dough (for baking), putty, sawdust, oatmeal, and papier mache offer children a variety of molding experiences.

Children can also participate in activities common in daily experiences to promote small muscle coordination—zipping, buttoning, sewing, screwing caps on small jars, screwing nuts and bolts, typing, tying knots and bows, and playing a piano. The art curriculum can enhance small muscle development with activities such as painting (with easel or larger brushes), coloring, drawing, sketching, tearing paper, folding paper, and for older children, cutting paper with scissors. Scissors are often introduced into the curriculum too early. Children can be seen struggling with scissors when tearing would be a more appropriate activity. The many forms of scissors designed to make cutting easier for young children make scissor use less of an indicator of competence in small muscle coordination than it has been in previous times.

A word is in order about the left-handed child. Approximately ten percent of the population is left-handed (Foerster 1975). The small muscle activities listed above will help each child develop hand dominance as well as provide opportunities for teachers to observe and respect the child's handedness. As instruction in letter formation is begun, it is recommended that left-handers be grouped together for instruction (Enstrom 1969).

Eye-Hand Coordination

The second kind of abilities children need in a strong early childhood handwriting program is eye-hand coordination. Competence in eye-hand coordination is related to small muscle development because children must have small muscle control to accomplish what the eye and brain wish to be done. Many of the small muscle activities mentioned above also enhance eye-hand coordination.

Any of the manipulative activities requiring utensils develop eye-hand coordination. Constructing with Legos, blocks, or popsicle sticks builds eye-hand coordination. Balancing objects such as blocks requires precise hand motions. Other precision motor activities include playing the piano, typing, working puzzles, stringing beads, weaving, sewing, using a calculator, and of course playing computer games. Even large muscle activities such as climbing a ladder, playing Simon Says, and jumping rope help build eye-hand coordination.

Copying is often part of a handwriting program. However, young children frequently have difficulty with far-to-near copying such as from a chalkboard or chart paper. Children's immature eyes have difficulty translating distant images to close-up images. It is better to have young children copy on paper with the same size letters as the model, first copying directly below the model, then copying from a model placed nearby. Copying should always be a choice activity for preschoolers to insure that only those children ready to copy participate.

Holding Utensils or Tools

Children need to manipulate tools as part of their early childhood curriculum. A water table with sponges, funnels, straws, and squeeze bottles is essential. Likewise, a sand table with sieves, strainers, containers of various sizes and shapes, sticks, shovels, and pails gives children opportunities to use tools.

Handwriting experiences can begin with markers and felt-tip pens. After the child gains confidence in making firm strokes while holding the tools in a relaxed manner (since they require little pressure), crayons and eventually pencils can be introduced. Crayons, often used as beginning writing tools, require more pressure than markers in order to produce the brighter colors to which children have become accustomed. There is no particular advantage to the large child-sized pencils. In fact, some children write better using

> It is important that children learn how to hold the writing tool properly from the beginning, because incorrect habits are difficult to break later.

regular adult-sized pencils from the start. A useful tool is a regular-sized pencil containing large soft lead. The Handy Grip triangular colored pencils and regular pencils make gripping the writing tool easy, resulting in smoother and more clear strokes. Although no research studies have involved preschoolers, there is evidence that older children write better with felt-tip and ballpoint pens than with pencils (Krzesni 1971).

It is important that children learn how to hold the writing tool properly from the beginning, because incorrect habits are difficult to break later. The pencil should be loosely gripped with the fingers above the shaved tip to about an inch from the tip. Only the index finger should remain on top of the pencil, not two or three fingers. Left-handers should be encouraged not to "hook" (Enstrom 1969). However, do not stress position of the pencil to such a degree that you discourage the young writers. Rather, simply provide a variety of tools for writing. The child naturally will seek those that are easier. Children who select pencils are ready for instruction on the correct position for holding that tool. If the triangular pencils are used, hand position is automatic and easily achieved.

Basic Strokes

A fourth ability that is needed prior to instruction in letter formation is the ability to form basic strokes smoothly, in the appropriate direction, and with clean intersections. Observe a child's drawings. Circles and straight lines occur naturally in children's drawings. Are the circles round and closed? Do the straight lines intersect properly in such cases as body parts attached to bodies, kites to strings, etc.? Until these strokes occur naturally in such drawings as wagons, cars and trucks, houses, people, flowers, etc., the child is not ready for formal handwriting instruction.

Activities in addition to drawing and painting that give children opportunities to use basic strokes include stirring, sand play, water play, and finger painting. It is important that children not be taught how to make basic strokes in their artwork, but rather that these strokes evolve through time and experience, enhancing creativity as well as handwriting. Basic strokes can then be "taught" as part of the handwriting curriculum. Wright and Allen (1975) recommend practice in basic strokes before formal writing begins, so correct sequence of strokes within letters and letter formation can be taught from the start. Teachers should supervise initial writing attempts to discourage the development of bad habits (Enstrom 1965).

The transition from drawing to handwriting is a slow one involving basic strokes in both artistic and written form. A number of principles can be used to identify children who are making the transition:

- Recurring principle—The child repeats patterns (or letters or words) over and over.

- Directional principle—The child goes from left to right and then return sweeps to begin again at the left.

- Generating principle—The child realizes that letter elements can recur in variable patterns.

- Inventory principle—The child lists all of the letters (or words or symbols) he or she knows.

- Contrastive principle—The child perceives likenesses and differences among letter elements, concepts, letters, and words (Clay 1975).

Not only is it important to observe as a child demonstrates each principle, but abundant drawing and writing experiences should be provided to support the child's acquisition of these principles.

Letter Perception

Sometimes handwriting is viewed solely as a physical activity demanding small muscle coordination with little visual perception. In a longitudinal study of children's handwriting development emphasizing the perceptual-motor nature of handwriting, Furner (1969a, 1969b, 1970) demonstrated that attention to perception in a handwriting program develops better writers than a conventional program.

Furner's program suggests that young children need to be able to recognize form, notice likenesses and differences, infer movement necessary to the production of form, and give accurate verbal descriptions of things they see. Children should observe the finished product (letter or word) as well as the formational act (adult writing the letter or word as a model). Left-handers need left-handed models (Foerster 1975). Self-correction of initial attempts at handwriting can also aid in the development of letter perception (Furner 1969a, 1969b).

> **The importance of adult modeling of proper letter formation cannot be overemphasized.**

It is best to use a standard form of manuscript printing initially to teach children to write alphabet letters. The importance of adult modeling of proper letter formation cannot be overemphasized. Have children use unlined paper at first. Children are ready for lines when their writing becomes linear and has a consistent height on a paper without lines. Children write no better on special wide-lined paper than they do on regular adult paper with narrow spaces for writing (Halpin & Halpin 1976).

Reversals occur frequently in the initial stages of handwriting. They usually disappear as children mature. Most reversals correspond to the overgeneralizations that children make when they are learning to talk, such as saying *runned* for the word *ran*. The child making this error is overgeneralizing the rule for forming past tense. Similarly, one generalization for handwriting is that you write from left to right. Letters with initial strokes that move from right to left (j and s, for example) counter this generalization and are typically reversed when children first learn how to write them.

Teachers can help solve reversal problems by (a) pointing out differences in direction and (b) giving practice dealing correctly with the symbols that cause difficulty (Reilly 1972). Children need to perceive visually the way letters are formed; so the more children see the teacher write (on paper just as the child will write), the better. Some letters cause reversal problems with nearly all children—**b** and **d, s,** and uppercase **N**; these need to be taught carefully with special attention to the correct beginning point, correct direction of motion, and correct sequence of multipart letters (Enstrom & Enstrom 1969).

Orientation to Printed Language

In many ways children develop as readers and writers simultaneously. For children to be able to handwrite, they need reasons for writing, concepts of communication, and an orientation to printed language. For children to become readers they likewise need reasons for reading, contexts for reading, and orientation to printed language. Clay (1975) describes components of orientation to printed language.

- How to attend and orient to printed language
- How to organize one's exploratory investigation of printed forms
- How to tell left from right
- How to visually analyze letters and words

Children can have all of the mechanical abilities to perform handwriting tasks, but unless they see the "whole"—what printed language stands for and how it is used to communicate—they will not likely have the motivation to develop good handwriting skills. Just as in reading, we must be careful to avoid subdividing handwriting instruction into minute subskills.

Herein lies the importance of incorporating numerous writing activities into the early childhood curriculum. Children need to make lots of books, greeting cards, pictures with labels, charts, maps, letters to mail, and signs while they are still scribbling and mock writing. Likewise, they need to "read" lots of favorite songs, stories, and rhymes from charts and class books that have been written in their presence. Each child can have a mailbox or cubby to encourage written communication even before learning to write formally. Handwriting ought not occur in isolation but rather should be an integral part of the oral and written language program.

Conclusion

It is important that all six perceptual and mechanical areas (small muscle development, eye-hand coordination, holding a writing tool, basic strokes, letter perception, and orientation to printed language) be included but not rushed in an early childhood curriculum. A planned curriculum such as the one outlined in this article, accompanied by an immersion in reading and writing activities, is necessary prior to formal handwriting instruction. Because children enter school with a wide repertoire of skills and abilities, early childhood teachers need to be able to assess individual differences and provide both informal handwriting activities for children who are not yet ready for formal handwriting instruction and careful beginning instruction for children who are ready.

Because some children learn to write at home and in preschool and many others receive at least some instruction from parents and preschool teachers, the handwriting curriculum should involve parents (Hall, Moretz, & Statom 1976). Teachers can help parents understand why young children should not be pushed into formal handwriting, but rather be allowed to emerge into handwriting with the support of a rich perceptual, motor, and writing curriculum. Ideas for helping their children with these curricular activities can be valuable as parents understand the importance of providing their children with many free writing and drawing opportunities. Because many parents do teach their children how to write, they will appreciate knowing how and when to get them off to a good start. The parent component of the early childhood handwriting curriculum is at least as important as (and may be more important than) the school curriculum.

References

Clay, M. (1975). *What did I write?* Portsmouth, NH: Heinemann.

Enstrom, E. (1965). Handwriting: Let's begin in kindergarten. *Catholic Educator 36*, 40-41.

Enstrom, E. (1969). The left-handed child. *Today's Education 58*, 43-44.

Enstrom, E. & Enstrom, C. (1969). In print handwriting: Preventing and solving reversal problems. *Elementary English 46*, 759-764.

Foerster, L. (1975). Sinistral power! Help for left-handed children. *Elementary English 52*, 213-215.

Furner, B. (1970). An analysis of the effectiveness of a program of instruction emphasizing the perceptual-motor nature of learning handwriting. *Elementary English 47*, 61-69.

Furner, B. (1969a). The perceptual-motor nature of learning in handwriting. *Elementary English 46,* 886-894.

Furner, B. (1969b). Recommended instructional procedures in a method emphasizing the perceptual-motor nature of learning in handwriting. *Elementary English 46,* 1021-1030.

Hall, M., Moretz, S., & Statom, J. (1976). Writing before grade one—A study of early writers. *Language Arts 53,* 582-585.

Hall, N. (1989). *Writing with reason: The emergence of authorship in young children.* Portsmouth, NH: Heinemann.

Hall, N. & Robinson, A. (1991). *"Some day you will no all about me,": Young children's explorations in the world of letters.* Portsmouth, NH: Heinemann.

Halpin, G. & Halpin, G. (1976). Special paper for beginning handwriting: An unjustified practice? *Journal of Educational Research 69,* 267-269.

Hubbard, R. (1989). *Authors of pictures, draughtsmen of words.* Portsmouth, NH: Heinemann.

Krzesni, J. (1971). Effect of different writing tools and paper on performance of the third graders. *Elementary English 48,* 821-824.

Lamme, L. (1985). *Growing up writing.* Washington, D.C.: Acropolis.

Olson, J. (1992). *Envisioning writing: Toward an integration of drawing and writing.* Portsmouth, NH: Heinemann.

Reilly, V. (1972). Reversals in writing: Some suggestions for teachers. *Teaching Exceptional Children 4,* 145-146.

Wright, J. & Allen, E. (1975). Ready to write! *Elementary School Journal 75,* 430-435.

An Excerpt From

Beginning to Read: Thinking and Learning About Print

Marilyn Jager Adams

After children have become thoroughly familiar
with the letters and their names, reading and
writing activities follow far more easily.

Summary: Learning Letters

Solid familiarity with the visual shapes of the individual letters is an
absolute prerequisite for learning to read. To make this assertion more
vivid, we may compare two "word"-learning studies, one by Peiter
Reitsma (1983) and one by Lee Brooks (1977).

Reitsma's study was undertaken with twenty-nine normal, second-
grade Dutch children. He presented each child with a list of ten
pseudowords, four to seven letters in length, and printed on cards.
Flipping through the cards, he gave each child four or eight tries, with
feedback, at reading each of the pseudowords.

Three days later, Reitsma measured the speed and accuracy with
which the children could read these same pseudowords, using two sets
of control items for comparison. One set of control items consisted of
homophonic pseudowords, spelled identically to the trained words with
the exception of one single (often visually confusable) letter. The other
set consisted of unrelated and previously unseen pseudowords whose
pronunciations the children had repeated during training.

Those who three days earlier had been given just four practice trials
read both the trained pseudowords and their homophonic contrasts significantly faster than the unrelated controls. Those who had practiced
eight times read the trained pseudowords faster than either the homophonic or unrelated controls. None of the children made many errors.

Reitsma then extended this study using a set of unfamiliar real
(Dutch) words, four to ten letters long, with eighteen normal first-grade
children. The words were again printed on cards but this time embed-
ded in meaningful sentences. The training sentences and, thus, the test
words they contained, were read two, four, or six times by each child.

Three days later, the training words, along with sets of homophonic and unrelated control words, were presented in isolation on a computer screen, and the children were timed as they read each aloud. After only two practice trials, both the trained words and their homophones were read significantly faster than the unrelated controls. After only four practice trials, the trained words were read significantly faster than either their homophonic or their unrelated controls.

Against this remarkably spongelike word acquisition of Reitsma's young children, we may compare the performance of a group of college students trained by Brooks (1977). Brooks's adult subjects were given twelve monosyllabic, four "letter" pseudowords to learn. The spellings of six of the pseudowords reflected frequent English spelling-to-sound rules. The spellings of the other six did not and therefore had to be learned as "whole word patterns." (In fact, Brooks's purpose in conducting this experiment was to compare the speed of phonic versus whole word learning.)

The two types of words were trained in separate blocks of trials so that there should have been little confusion as to which were and which were not alphabetically decodable. With

> **Solid familiarity with the visual shapes of the individual letters is an absolute prerequisite for learning to read.**

respect to differences in the learnability of the two types of pseudowords, the alphabetic items showed a slight disadvantage early in training and a slight advantage later in training. However, the point here is that, after 200 practice trials with each of the twelve items, the adults were still having trouble recognizing them. Their learning curves were still not close to asymptote.

Two trials for the children versus hundreds for the adults: To what can we attribute this contrast? Whereas Reitsma's items were spelled with normal familiar letters, Brooks's were spelled with an invented alphabet. Brooks's characters were exceedingly simple—∞, ∨, −, |||, ∩, ⊔; there were only six of them; and the subjects were given ten minutes of practice just on the individual letter-sound correspondences before training began. Nevertheless, Brooks's adults, in contrast with Reitsma's children, had to learn to recognize—and to recognize easily—not just the sequences of characters of which each item was comprised but also the characters themselves.

The Orthographic processor cannot begin to learn spellings until it has learned to recognize the letters from which they must be built. The

Phonological processor cannot usefully learn letter sounds until the Orthographic processor has learned to discriminate the individual letters with which they must be linked. Yet the visual forms of the individual letters are abstract and highly confusable.

In view of this, I urge that instruction in letter recognition be begun long before children get to school. The goal is to ensure that the letter shapes are highly familiar and discriminable to the children before they are faced with the tasks of learning the letters' sounds or, more generally, of learning to read words. After children have become thoroughly familiar with the letters and their names, reading and writing activities follow far more easily.

Many preschoolers become familiar with letters through a common sequence of activities. First, they learn the alphabet song. Then they learn the shapes that go with each of the letter names they have learned. In both of these challenges, they may gain both motivation and guidance from "Sesame Street," especially if it is treated as a participatory program rather than passively watched. More generally, there is no substitute for the attention and praise of a real person in any enrichment activity.

For children who enter school with such background, there would seem to be little argument for avoiding careful use of letter names in the classroom. For children who enter school without it, however, this issue is more difficult. For these children, there is good reason for concern that distinctions between the names and sounds of letters will be confused if they are taught at the same time.

Both theory and data suggest that instruction on neither the sounds of letters nor the recognition of whole words should be earnestly undertaken until the child has become confident and quick at recognizing individual letters.[1] While *every* aspect of reading growth depends on the speed and accuracy of letter perception, learning to recognize and discriminate printed letters is just too big, too hard, and too fussy a task to be mastered incidentally, in tandem with some other hard and fussy task, or without an adult's focused attention to its progress and difficulties. Succinctly, what a waste to correct the pronunciation of a letter sound or word if the child's confusion was really in the visual identity of the letter.

---

[1] This is not to say that, before this, one should avoid showing printed words to children and helping them to appreciate that they symbolize spoken words, that they are comprised of individual letters, and that the letters correspond to the sounds of the corresponding words. This sort of exposure and the "print appreciation" it supports are key steps toward reading readiness.

Thus, even for poorly prepared children, I would be tempted to begin with the alphabet song. I would exploit the letter names it teaches along with any other kinds of appropriately challenging and interesting activities toward helping them learn the letters' shapes. Only after I was very sure that the children's learning of letter shapes was well under way, would I begin serious instruction in spelling-sound relations or word recognition.

It also seems like a good idea to exercise children's ability to print individual letters from the start. This is not only because of its potential for enhancing individual letter recognition but, further, because it will allow them to write words as soon as they are introduced—and, as we shall see, writing seems a solidly productive activity for the young reader.

In the initial introduction of a letter shape, and otherwise to assist development of fine motor skills, tracing may be used. Tracing exercises may be more effective if the stencils are coded to encourage a uniform sequence of motor patterns for each letter

> ...it appears that neither tracing nor copying, but independent printing holds the greatest leverage for perceptual and motor learning of letter shapes.

(e.g., for the letter **b**, first trace the vertical bar from top to bottom, then draw the circle). This is both because control develops through repetition and because it enhances the chances that the child will attend to the individual features of the letters and their interrelations. (Note that the basis of this recommendation is orthogonal to any puritanical notions about the hygiene of penpersonship. After the children have thoroughly learned the letters, it is okay if they want to write them in a mirror, with their toes, while standing on their heads.)

Copying, of course, must be used; it is a necessary step toward the independent printing of a letter. But it appears that neither tracing nor copying, but independent printing holds the greatest leverage for perceptual and motor learning of letter shapes. It will be obvious when a child needs a model to produce a letter—that is, it will be obvious when reversion to copying is necessary. In such cases, copying should be encouraged and coupled with guidance about those aspects of the letter with which the child is having difficulty.

It also seems that whenever letter-sound instruction is begun, it is a good idea to present integrated letter/keyword/picture displays. These may be charts to be hung on the classroom wall or pictures in an alphabet book. In whatever showcase, such displays provide mnemonic assistance for letter shapes, letter sounds, and their couplings, at once.

Finally, given that the notion that letters spell words is so very critical, one wonders why more preschool trade books and preprimers are not produced in ways that make their print more salient. In tradebooks, at least, the possibilities of graphically or stylistically enhancing print are myriad. Again, some of Dr. Seuss's books provide good models. Further, one wonders why so very few preschool tradebooks and preprimers are printed in uppercase type. Inasmuch as children generally learn uppercase letters first, this might provide a good early clue that letters are related to language and print.

References

Brooks, L. (1977). Visual pattern in fluent word identification. In A.S. Reber and D.L. Scarborough (eds.), *Toward a psychology of reading*, 143-181. Hillsdale, NJ: Erlbaum Associates.

Reitsma, P. (1983). Printed word learning in beginning readers. *Journal of Experimental Child Psychology, 36*, 321-339.

"If you don't learn to sign your name smaller it'll never fit on checks."

Reprinted with special permission of King Features Syndicate.

The Effect of Handwriting Style on Alphabet Recognition

Debby Kuhl and Peter Dewitz

Some kindergarten children in my classroom appeared
to struggle with learning the alphabet, and regular recording
of their errors suggested that the D'Nealian alphabet might be
a possible cause of their problem.

For too long education has operated like the fashion industry. We allow ourselves to be influenced by passing fads and outside sources. This is a dangerous practice because our mistakes affect what and how children learn. Today curriculum is influenced by everyone from parents to publishers and while these influences have their place, we must be sure what happens in school is based on sound educational research. This research demonstrates how one such mistake may be affecting early readers all across the country.

Over a decade ago many school systems, including ours, adopted D'Nealian manuscript (Thurber, 1984) (also published as Modern Manuscript by other publishers) for writing instruction. Developed by Donald Thurber and published by Scott Foresman, the program was introduced into twenty-three states and is now widely used. This print form seemed perfectly logical because it made the transition from man-uscript to cursive writing easier. Research on the D'Nealian form of handwriting has focused on the ease of stroke production, and there is no conclusive evidence that D'Nealian is superior to standard manu-script even though that was the goal of its creator (Connell, 1983; Duvall, 1985). The shortcoming of this well-intentioned practice was that it fails to take into consideration a critical aspect of print instruc-tion: its potential effect on letter recognition. Only one study could be found on the relationship of letter recognition and handwriting style, and this study, with only 12 students, found that D'Nealian handwriting had no negative effects on the number of letter reversals when reading D'Nealian print, but other recognition problems were ignored (Thurber, 1984). The study did not examine the effect of D'Nealian handwriting on the letter recognition of traditional manuscript handwriting. Since letter recognition is one of the most critical skills for early readers' success, having difficulty with this skill can have a damaging impact on early reading achievement.

As my kindergarten students began to learn the alphabet and learned to write, I noticed problems they had learning to recognize letters. They consistently had difficulty identifying several letters, often making the same erroneous response to the same letter. As I recorded all responses in an attempt to analyze what they were doing, I began to notice patterns from child to child. D'Nealian manuscript appeared to be harder to learn. After collaborating with other kindergarten teachers in our district kindergarten center, I found their experiences were similar. I suspected that there was some relationship to our use of D'Nealian manuscript and the children's difficulty with letter recognition because the students appeared more successful when the letters were printed in the traditional form. I began to explore the research in an effort to understand the processes involved in learning letter names.

The D'Nealian alphabet was designed to smooth the transition from manuscript printing to cursive writing. Figure 1 presents some of the differences between D'Nealian and traditional handwriting, or the Zaner-Bloser style (Barbe, Wasylyk, Hackney, and Braun, 1984). D'Nealian manuscript uses a continuous stroke production with a slight slant. An upswing stroke has been added to **a, d, h, i, l, m, n, t, u,** and **x.** The letters w and y are formed by joined curves rather than joined lines. The letter k has a closed arc added. The traditional print is perpendicular to and ends at the baseline except for descending letters.

> **Since letter recognition is one of the most critical skills for early readers' success, having difficulty with this skill can have a damaging impact on early reading achievement.**

Grapheme awareness or letter-name knowledge is an essential skill in early reading. It has been demonstrated by Chall (1967), Bond and Dykstra (1967), and others to be the best predictor of early reading achievement (Adams, 1991). While the predictive quality does not suggest that simple letter knowledge produces subsequent reading success, it does suggest that this knowledge is fundamental to the reading process.

As children learn to read, letter-name knowledge is an important aid to word recognition. When children abandon their logographic style of word recognition and move toward alphabetic reading, a stage called visual cue reading (Ehri, 1991), they use letter names as access routes for word identification (Scott and Ehri, 1990). The letter name is the cue by which the word is identified. Next, letter names provide the first cue as to the sounds of the letters. Many letter names begin with a phoneme that is also the sound most frequently represented by that letter, as in **b** and **t**, but not **w**. Later, during alphabetic reading, accurate letter recognition is essential to learning letter/sound association. Skill at alphabetic reading is necessary in order to become proficient at orthographic processing (Firth, 1985). In a sense, orthographic processing matures from letter-by-letter encoding used by kindergarten students to holistic word reading or spelling patterns by second grade (Juola, Schadler, Chabot, and McCaughey, 1977). In regard to all these processes one must conclude that letter knowledge, along with phoneme awareness, is an essential skill underlying all stages of word recognition. Even the mature reader looks at almost every word on a page and also processes most letters (McConkie and Zola, 1981). Simply stated, readers must process individual letters at some level before word recognition can become automatic. The amount of attention

> **This study will discuss the perceptual processes involved in letter recognition and demonstrate how D'Nealian manuscript inhibits letter recognition both in theory and practice.**

required to process individual letters will ultimately inhibit or facilitate word recognition. This study will discuss the perceptual processes involved in letter recognition and demonstrate how D'Nealian manuscript inhibits letter recognition both in theory and practice.

Gibson (1969) theorized that perception involved three types of learning: the ability to perceive distinctive features, the identification of invariant properties, and the formation of higher order structures or the relationship of the features to the whole. Distinctive features are the properties of stimuli that distinguish one from another, the lines, curves, and intersections (Gibson and Levin, 1975). The capital letter **E** is distinguished from the capital **F** by one distinctive feature, a horizontal line. Gibson found that the letters that shared many distinctive features, e.g., **P** and **R**, were more frequently confused than were letters that shared few or no distinctive features, e.g., **X** and **O** (Gibson, Gibson, Pick, and Osser, 1963).

To understand why these confusions existed, a cluster analysis was done to determine the significance of specific features. The single most important feature attended to by both children and adults was the straight-curved attribute. (The letters **b** and **d** embody both attributes.) This was followed by letters without intersection (e.g., **O**), curved letters with intersection (e.g., **C**), then letters with diagonality (e.g., **N**) (Gibson and Levin, 1975). Not only does this identification process demonstrate the importance of attention to attributes, but it also suggests that these attributes need to be consistent. The learner must know which feature is characteristic of a specific letter symbol or symbols.

The D'Nealian manuscript alters the distinctive features of letters. Many D'Nealian letters are written with curves thus eliminating the most important feature, the straight-curved attribute. D'Nealian adds features

> **The D'Nealian manuscript alters the distinctive features of letters.**

to letters that are not present in traditional manuscript, also making the perceptual process more difficult. **Y** is written with a curve, making it look like a traditional **g,** and a closed arc is added to the **k,** making it resemble a capital **R** in traditional handwriting. The **w** is changed to joined curves making it look like a traditional but inverted **m.**

As children learn the D'Nealian manuscript, they are also exposed to the traditional manuscript letterforms in books and environmental print. But perceptual learning, at least at first, requires an invariant model. This is the idea that learning occurs because certain things are static and the relation of the events is invariant over time and context (Gibson, 1975). Mature readers can deal with invariant models as they encounter many different type fonts. In all learning, sensory input is needed, but it is only when the input is repetitive and predictable that concepts are formed.

Learning letter symbols is a result of attending to predictable distinctive features and requires those features to be invariant. This is particularly important because most children receive formal letter instruction in kindergarten at a time when they are in a preoperational thought stage. At this stage they may be incapable of attending to both the similarities and differences of two letter types or unable to make transformations from one state to another (Kirkland, 1978). This would be confusing as they attempted to make sense of letterforms presented by the teacher in D'Nealian and other manuscript forms encountered in books and environmental print. This would also likely reduce their ability to make natural connections between the letter names and the graphic features. When the D'Nealian forms are compared to Zaner-Bloser forms (Barbe et al., 1975), the source of the confusion becomes more apparent. The D'Nealian lowercase k looks like a traditional uppercase **R,** and the D'Nealian lowercase l resembles the traditional uppercase J if the child fails to note the orientation of the letter and makes a reversal.

The last perceptual process involved in letter symbol acquisition is the formation of higher order structures. This is the ability of the learner to reflect on contrastive features of the parts to the whole. They must be able to understand the whole is formed by the relationship of the subordinate features and make judgments concerning relevant and irrelevant sensory information. Thus perception begins with maximum contrasts and progresses to smaller ones (Gibson and Levin, 1975). It is hypothesized that this ability is transferred when learning object discrimination. This explains why children have difficulty with the reversal, rotational, and perspective qualities of letter symbols, as in the recognition of **b, d, p,** and **q** in traditional manuscript. This is the first time the identity of something is changed as a result of its position. The ability to make contrastive judgments was found to be developmental in nature with declines in errors noted between ages four and eight. The greatest decline was in the perception of reversal rotational patterns, followed by line to curve, and then perspective judgments (Gibson and Levin, 1975).

The D'Nealian manuscript demands that the young learner make additional perceptual judgments about the orientation of letters in space. The added upswing strokes increase the frequency of letter reversals, line to curve, and perspective judgments required by the new distinctive features. The addition of the upswing stroke to the D'Nealian lowercase i makes it likely that the young reader will confuse the letter with the lowercase j; a new piece of relevant sensory information has been introduced. The addition of a new distinctive feature increases the likelihood of a rotational error.

> **Perceptual learning theory suggests that the D'Nealian manuscript by itself is harder to learn than traditional manuscript....**

Perceptual learning theory suggests that the D'Nealian manuscript by itself is harder to learn than traditional manuscript and that the teaching of D'Nealian manuscript interferes with the children's recognition of traditional manuscript, which is most common in the natural school environment. Since letter recognition is often an early indication of future reading problems (Adams, 1991; Clay, 1983), the weaker students should be more at risk when learning the D'Nealian alphabet than weaker students who learn only the traditional manuscript forms. It was because of the underlying importance of letter recognition and the problems we experienced that a comparative study was done. This study examines the letter recognition abilities of two groups of kindergarten children. One group was taught the traditional manuscript (Zaner-Bloser) and the other the D'Nealian manuscript.

Methods
Subjects

The subjects were 100 kindergarten boys and girls from two suburban schools. Fifty subjects were randomly sampled from the total kindergarten population of each school. The two schools were equal on two socio-economic indices. Each school served a middle-class population and each had a small but equal percentage of students on free and reduced lunch programs. In the D'Nealian school 5.4% of the students qualified for a free or reduced lunch, and in the traditional manuscript school 4.7% of the students qualified.

The subjects were categorized into low, average, and high ability students. In the school using D'Nealian, the classification was based on student stanine scores on the May Metropolitan Reading Readiness Test. In the school using traditional alphabet instruction, the classification was based on teacher evaluation of related classroom performance. No standardized test is given in this school to kindergarten students.

Classroom Instruction

Alphabet instruction in both schools began in the fall of the year and focused on a letter of the week. Both programs included multi-sensory experiences with the alphabet and introduced sound symbol correspondence rules. In the traditional print school, the students received the visual models of the letters on wall charts, manipulatives, big books, worksheets, and teacher-made materials. In the D'Nealian print school, the children used the D'Nealian model on alphabet charts, teacher-made materials, language experience writing, and worksheets. They were also exposed to traditional print in big books, manipulatives, and library books, as those materials are often not available in D'Nealian print. Neither school emphasized formal handwriting instruction in kindergarten, but the teachers demonstrated the correct stroke production as children used the letters in their writing.

Experimental Procedures

The children's knowledge of the alphabet was measured in late May after both schools had completed alphabet instruction. The subjects were evaluated by the same individual during the same calendar week. Each student read the alphabet from two sets of 3" x 5" cards with one set of cards printed in the D'Nealian alphabet and the other set printed in the traditional alphabet. The stimuli on the cards were photocopied lowercase letters taken from commercially prepared alphabet charts of both print styles. The cards were presented one type style at a time in random order, alternating the order of presentation for print style after each subject. The cards within each stack were also shuffled following each presentation in order to insure the letter order remained random. The response of each subject was recorded as given. If children failed to give a response or stated that they didn't know, the response was recorded as "doesn't know."

Results

The kindergarten students were tested on their knowledge of the D'Nealian and traditional alphabets. The first analysis was a 2(school) x 2(handwriting style) x 2(sex) x 3(Ability) x 2(order of presentation) Analysis of Variance with number of recognition errors as the dependent variable. The means and standard deviations are presented in Table 1. The results of the Analysis of Variance yielded a main effect for handwriting style $F(1,94) = 24.556$, $p < .001$ with all children producing more errors when reading the D'Nealian (M = 4.78) compared to the traditional alphabet (M = 1.70). There was also a main effect for Ability, $F(2,94) = 10.323$, $p < .001$, with recognition accuracy directly related to general reading readiness. There was no main effect for School $F(1,94) = 1.692$, $p > .05$, Sex $F(1,94) = 1.559$, $p > .05$, or order of presentation $F(1,94) = 1.012$, $p > .05$. There was also a significant School by Handwriting Style interaction $F(2,94) = 4.240$, $p < .01$. Students in the school where traditional handwriting is taught had fewer errors in recognizing the traditional alphabet (M = .72) than they did with the D'Nealian system (M = 5.44). The same was true for the children in the D'Nealian school. Children taught using the D'Nealian alphabet made fewer errors on traditional print (M = 2.68) than they did on D'Nealian print (M = 4.12). However, the students in the traditional school were better on traditional print than were the students in the D'Nealian school.

Finally, there was an Ability by School by Handwriting style inter-action $F(3,94) = 7.15$, $p < .01$. This interaction is illustrated in Figure 2. High ability kindergartners who are taught the D'Nealian handwriting style perform equally well on the recognition of both traditional and D'Nealian alphabets. Average and low ability students who are taught the D'Nealian handwriting style perform better on the traditional alphabet than they do on the D'Nealian alphabet, but the ability to recognize the traditional alphabet is hampered when compared to their counterparts who have been taught the traditional alphabet.

In the second analysis, error frequencies for individual letters were calculated, and a confusion matrix was generated to determine the kinds of perceptual confusion that children experience with the two different handwriting systems. The error frequencies are presented in Table 2. When reading the traditional alphabet, the kindergarten students in the traditional class-rooms made the most number of errors on letters that share the most distinctive features. Thus there were a substantial number of errors on **b**, **d**, and **q**, as is normally expected because they are reversal-rotational errors. The letters **b** and **d** caused the most difficulty with 9 errors and 8 errors respectively.

> **When children in D'Nealian classrooms read the traditional alphabet, new errors occurred.**

When children in D'Nealian classrooms read the traditional alpha-bet, new errors occurred. In addition to the difficulty with **b**, **d**, and **q**, errors were also made on the letters **f**, **g**, **j**, **l**, and **u**. Twenty students made errors on the letter **l**, 10 on the letter **j**, and 9 on the letter **g**. The responses to **l** and **j** reveal the influence of the D'Nealian system. The errors on the traditional **l** and **j** were made by students in the D'Nealian classrooms who read these letters as **i**. In the D'Nealian alphabet, **i** and **j** have the same distinctive features and only differ because the letters are reversals of one another. The distinctive features of **i** and **j** are carried over from the D'Nealian alphabet and cause confusion in learning the traditional alphabet.

The D'Nealian alphabet causes confusion even for those students who are taught it and must recognize it. The confusion the D'Nealian students have is presented in Figure 3, a confusion matrix. In the

D'Nealian alphabet, **b** and **d** still caused considerable letter confusion, but additional problems occurred on **i, j, k, u, w, y**, and **g**. The letter **k** in D'Nealian handwriting illustrates the problem for the children. In the D'Nealian handwriting, an arc is added to the **k** making it resemble the capital **R** in the traditional system. The letter **k** is rarely confused with other letters in the traditional alphabet, but in D'Nealian it shares features with **R** and was misread by almost half of the students in the study. Additional confusion exists between **w** and **m** and **y** and **g** because the distinctive features are more similar in D'Nealian than in traditional print.

When the students in the traditional classroom read the D'Nealian alphabet, their error patterns were very similar to the D'Nealian students. They made the most number of errors on letters that were also difficult for the D'Nealian students. However, the traditional students were more successful on the D'Nealian **g, h**, and **j** than were their counterparts in the D'Nealian classroom. In the traditional alphabet, the **j** has the features of a curve and a dot, whereas in the D'Nealian alphabet, the **i** has the same features. The traditional students were never exposed to the D'Nealian **i**; therefore, they had no potential source of confusion.

Discussion

In this study I set out to demonstrate that handwriting style has a significant effect on letter recognition. The research question was generated from classroom experiences and personal observation. Some kindergarten children in my classroom appeared to struggle with learning the alphabet, and regular recording of their errors suggested that the D'Nealian alphabet might be a possible cause of their problem.

The data reveals that D'Nealian manuscript causes more confusion than does traditional manuscript and interferes with the ability of students in D'Nealian classrooms to read traditional print. It is important that the early reader be taught a handwriting style that minimizes confusion. The present study demonstrates that D'Nealian manuscript is not only harder to learn than traditional print, but D'Nealian creates substantially more letter recognition errors and causes more letter confusion than does the traditional style. One of the foundations of word recognition is the ability to recognize the printed symbols of our alphabet. It is the interplay of those individual letters that constitute words, and words communicate meaning. If the individual letters cause confusion, then word recognition is likely to be impeded, as is early reading development. The attention of early readers should not be distracted by print variation.

The D'Nealian manuscript makes letter recognition harder for all students, and the problem is especially critical for the weaker students in kindergarten. Low-achieving students are dramatically affected by D'Nealian manuscript and are being impaired in learning the skill fundamental to the reading process, i.e., letter recognition. In comparing the two schools, not only were the low-achieving students more affected, but the error rate for low-achieving students taught D'Nealian and tested with D'Nealian was alarming (M = 8.17) in comparison to the low-achieving students taught traditional print and tested with traditional print (M = 1.56).

> Low-achieving students are dramatically affected by D'Nealian manuscript and are being impaired in learning the skill fundamental to the reading process, i.e., letter recognition.

Learning the D'Nealian manuscript style also poses problems for the high-achieving students. For many high-achieving students who may come to kindergarten with letter knowledge, we spend time reteaching the letters to be consistent with our handwriting style, even though traditional print recognition will be needed for reading. This is a waste of instructional time and a cause of confusion to many children. Considering the negative impact of the D'Nealian manuscript style, we must seriously question the positive gains, i.e., easy transition to cursive writing and fluid stroke production. This is a problem of costs and benefits. The benefits of promoting cursive handwriting and fluid stroke production are probably not outweighed by the negative costs of letter recognition problems. To solidify this conclusion, the kindergarten students who are learning D'Nealian handwriting should be watched as they proceed into first grade and their word recognition ability should be studied.

A limitation of the study was the inability to randomly assign students to treatments, but this was almost impossible. The choice of handwriting style is typically a school district decision, and children cannot be randomly assigned to school districts. The study does illustrate the power of research questions that are generated by classroom teachers who notice student learning patterns and question instructional practices.

If the foundation of word recognition lies in the ability to recognize the printed symbols of our alphabet, we must choose instructional practices that build the strongest possible foundation. The amount of attention required to learn and process letters will ultimately inhibit or facilitate word recognition and early reading success. While there is considerable debate about how to teach beginning reading, almost all of this debate revolves around methods of reading instruction. A review of the literature indicates that nobody has ever considered manuscript handwriting style as a factor in learning to recognize letters and an aspect of beginning reading.

The present study further points to the problems that may occur when educational innovations are adopted without careful research and evaluation. The developers of D'Nealian manuscript style document its effectiveness by citing research on how the D'Nealian style makes stroke production easier (Thurber, 1984). The research failed to consider the impact of handwriting style on letter recognition.

TABLE I. Mean and standard deviation of letter recognition errors

| | Traditional Alphabet | | D'Nealian Alphabet | |
	Traditional School	D'Nealian School	Traditional School	D'Nealian School
High Ability	.23 (.59)	1.28 (1.67)	3.6 (1.79)	1.50 (1.61)
Average Ability	.68 (.86)	2.73 (3.43)	5.52 (1.92)	5.00 (4.17)
Low Ability	1.56 (1.23)	6.67 (3.83)	6.56 (1.13)	8.17 (3.81)
Total	.72 (.96)	2.69 (3.34)	5.22 (2.01)	4.12 (4.02)

TABLE 2. Frequency of letter recognition errors

	Traditional Alphabet		D'Nealian Alphabet	
	Traditional Students	D'Nealian Students	Traditional Students	D'Nealian Students
a	0	8	6	5
b	9	11	14	11
c	2	2	4	2
d	8	18	11	14
e	0	2	2	2
f	1	6	1	6
g	2	9	4	12
h	0	5	1	9
i	1	2	43	22
j	1	10	4	15
k	2	1	35	12
l	3	20	43	31
m	0	3	2	1
n	1	4	3	7
o	0	0	3	0
p	0	2	5	1
q	3	9	14	12
r	1	3	3	3
s	2	0	4	0
t	0	0	8	5
u	2	7	19	12
v	0	4	2	6
w	1	2	12	9
x	0	2	7	2
y	2	3	25	12
z	1	0	2	3
Total Errors	42	133	277	214

FIGURE I. A comparison of D'Nealian and Zaner-Bloser manuscript

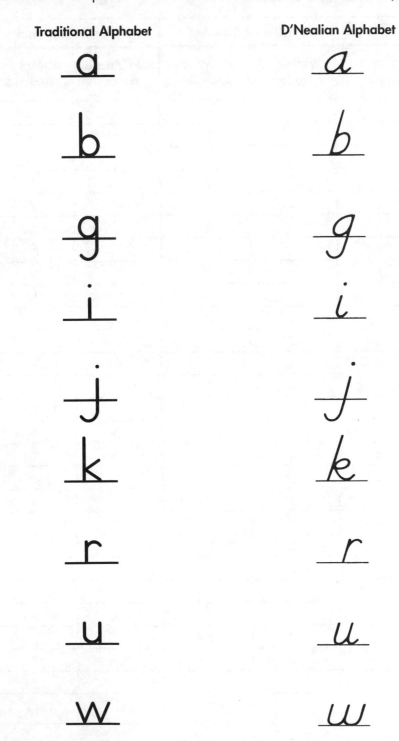

Traditional Alphabet   D'Nealian Alphabet

Vertical manuscript: Appropriate for beginning readers and writers?

FIGURE 2.

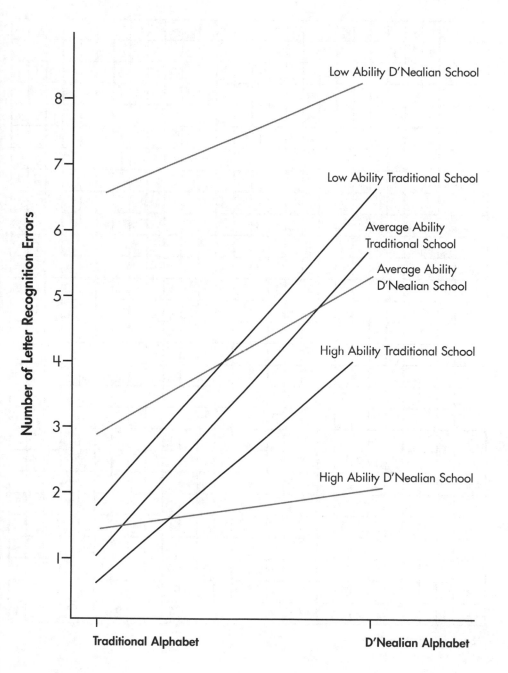

FIGURE 3. Error matrix for D'Nealian manuscript

	a	b	c	d	e	f	g	h	i	j	k	l	m	n	o	p	q	r	s	t	u	v	w	x	y	z
a		1		3										1			1									
b	2		6																							
c																										
d		7	1						1																	
e												1										1				
f																				1						
g			1														3								4	
h							2		1			1		3				1								
i										13	3															
j			1				3		19			22						1								
k			1																					1		
l			1						2		1						1									
m																					2		4		1	
n	1			1			8														2	1			1	1
o																										
p	1	1		2								1					2				1					
q							2																	1		
r		2						1	9		1					1										
s																										
t				1	2								1													
u																							1		3	
v				1									1								3	1				
w							1										1					1				
x																										
y							1										2				1	1				1
z							1																		1	
*	1					2	3			1	2	2	1	1			2	3			2	4	2	3	2	1

*Student did not know

References

Adams, M.J. (1991). *Beginning to Read, Thinking and Learning about Print.* MIT Press, Cambridge, MA.

Barbe, W.B., Milone, M., and Wasylyk, T.M. (1983). Manuscript is the "Write" Start. *Academic Therapy, 18,* 397-404.

Barbe, W.B., Wasylyk, T.M., Hackney, C.S., and Braun, L.A. (1984). *Zaner-Bloser Creative Growth in Handwriting (Grades K-8).* Columbus, OH: Zaner-Bloser.

Bond, G.L. and Dykstra, R. (1967). The cooperative research program in early reading instruction. *Reading Research Quarterly, 2,* 5-142.

Chall, J.S. (1967). *Learning to Read: The Great Debate.* New York: McGraw-Hill.

Clay, M. (1983). *Early Detection of Reading Difficulties.* Aukland, NZ: Heinemann.

Connell, D. (1983). Handwriting: Taking a look at alternatives. *Academic Therapy, 18,* 413-420.

Duvall, B. (1985). Evaluating the difficulty of four handwriting styles used for instruction. *ERS Spectrum, 3,* 13-18.

Firth, U. (1985). Beneath the surface of developmental dyslexia. In K.E. Patterson, J.C. Marshall, and M. Coltheart (Eds.) *Surface Dyslexia* (pp. 301-330). London: Erlbaum.

Gibson, E.J. (1969). *Principles of Perceptual Learning and Development.* New York: Prentice-Hall.

Gibson, E.J., Gibson, J.J., Pick, A.D., and Osser, H.A. (1962). A developmental study of the discrimination of letter like forms. *Journal of Comparative and Physiological Psychology, 55,* 897-906.

Gibson, E.J. and Levin, H. (1975). *The Psychology of Reading.* Cambridge, MA: The MIT Press.

Juola, J.F., Schadler, M., Chabot, R.J., and McCaughey, S. (1979). The development of visual information processing skills related to reading. *Journal of Experimental Psychology, 25,* 459-476.

Kirkland, E. (1978). A Piagetian interpretation of beginning reading instruction. *The Reading Teacher, 32,* 497-503.

McConkie, G.W. and Zola, D. (1981). Language constraints and the functional stimulus in reading. In A.M. Lesgold and C.A. Perfetti (Eds.) *Interactive processes in reading* (pp. 155-175). Hillsdale, NJ: Erlbaum.

Scott, J.A. and Ehri, L.C. (1990). Sight word reading in prereaders: Use of logographic vs. alphabetic access routes. *Journal of Reading Behavior, 22,* 149-166.

Thurber, D.N. (1984). *D'Nealian Manuscript: A Continuous Stroke Approach to Handwriting.* Novato, CA: Academic Therapy Publications.

Are Slanted Manuscript Alphabets Superior to the Traditional Manuscript Alphabet?

Steve Graham

Given the lack of supportive evidence and the practical problems involved in implementation, slanted manuscript letters cannot be recommended as a replacement of the traditional manuscript alphabet.

On "Back to School" night, a 1st-grade teacher was sharing with parents her plans for their children during the first half of the year. When one parent asked about handwriting, the teacher eagerly noted that they would be using the D'Nealian handwriting program (Thurber, 1993a).

The teacher went on to explain that the D'Nealian program did not use the traditional manuscript alphabet, which is characterized by round, upright letters that resemble type. Instead, they would use a modified script in which the manuscript letters are slanted and most of the "small" or lower-case letters resemble their cursive counterparts. She then showed the parents a chart containing the D'Nealian alphabet, emphasizing that the modified manuscript letters make the transition between manuscript and cursive writing easier and quicker for young children.

While most of the parents were unfamiliar with the D'Nealian alphabet or the concept of slanted manuscript letters, only a few voiced any comments. One parent noted that it seemed like a waste of time to learn a new script when her child could already write most of the traditional letters "quite well." Another parent, however, indicated that her older child had learned to write using D'Nealian, and that it was "simply marvelous." After hearing the first two comments, a third parent asked the teacher to "please tell us again why you think this new alphabet is better."

The teacher related many of the claims made by advocates for the newer, slanted manuscript style (Coon & Palmer, 1993; Thurber, 1993b). She reiterated that the new, slanted manuscript alphabet made the transition to cursive writing easier, saving a considerable amount of instructional time. She further indicated that the new, slanted alphabets, such as D'Nealian, used continuous strokes to form manuscript letters, resulting in better rhythm, greater speed, more writing and fewer letter reversals. She also stressed that this type of alphabet was better for children with learning disabilities and other handicaps.

> One parent noted that it seemed like a waste of time to learn a new script when her child could already write most of the traditional letters "quite well."

As she repeated and expanded her rationale, the teacher did not refer to the research that addresses whether slanted manuscript alphabets are superior to the traditional ones. And none of the parents thought to request evidence to support the claims. This paper examines the merits of the claims made by this 1st-grade teacher and the other advocates of slanted manuscript alphabets.

Background

Prior to the 1980s, the most critical issue involving handwriting script centered on whether to teach both manuscript and cursive writing. Some educators challenged the desirability of teaching both types of writing, recommending that only manuscript be taught (Groff, 1964; Templin, 1963) or making the more controversial suggestion that only cursive be taught (cf. Early, 1973). Neither of these recommendations generated enough support to seriously challenge the traditional approach of teaching manuscript in kindergarten through grade 2 and cursive in grade 2 or 3. Advocates of teaching only manuscript were unable to overcome tradition. Proponents for the cursive-only approach were unable to effectively counter evidence that manuscript writing is more legible than cursive writing, leads to greater gains in reading achievement, can be written as fast and is easier to learn (Askov & Peck, 1982; Graham & Miller, 1980).

During the 1980s, this debate declined in the United States and educators turned their attention to other styles of print (Askov & Peck, 1982), such as italics and the D'Nealian alphabet developed by Donald Thurber (1983). Interest in the use of alternative alphabets as a means to facilitate the transition to cursive writing was strong enough that two publishing companies developed handwriting programs that centered around the concept of slanted manuscript letters—the D'Nealian method, published by Scott, Foresman (Thurber, 1993a), and the McDougal, Littell (1993) program.

The development and commercialization of slanted manuscript alphabets has been accompanied by a variety of enthusiastic and optimistic claims regarding their superiority over traditional print (cf. Coon & Palmer, 1993; Thurber, 1983). While the issues surrounding the comparative effectiveness of slanted manuscript alphabets are relatively simple and straightforward, evaluation of supporters' claims has been complicated by three factors.

First, advocates for the new, slanted manuscript alphabets have made a surprisingly large number of frivolous claims (Graham, 1992). For example, supporters typically fail to make a distinction between claims for slanted alphabets and claims for the

> ...advocates for the new, slanted manuscript alphabets have made a surprisingly large number of frivolous claims.

methods used to teach them (cf. Ourada, 1993; Thurber, 1993a). Although the procedures used to teach the alphabet are important, they do not justify using a particular style of script.

Second, an emotional and almost evangelistic fervor has at times characterized the debate, further clouding the issues. Supporters of slanted manuscript alphabets often use the provocative phrase "ball and stick" to describe traditional manuscript (cf. Coon & Palmer, 1993). Also, the developer of the D'Nealian alphabet (Thurber, 1983) indicated that traditional manuscript "resulted in schools producing a nation of rather poor writers" (p.3), and that this style of printing may hinder beginning reading development. Evidence to support this claim, however, does not exist.

Third, there has been very little scientific interest in slanted manuscript alphabets and all the studies that have examined their effectiveness contained methodological problems. Almost uniformly, researchers have failed to control for differences in teaching methodology when studying the effectiveness of slanted versus traditional manuscript alphabets. In the typical experiment, one group of students is taught slanted manuscript letters using the Scott, Foresman handwriting program, while traditional manuscript is taught via the popular Zaner-Bloser handwriting program (Hackney & Lucas, 1993).

Any conclusions regarding the effects of manuscript style in these studies must be tempered, therefore, by the confounding influence of teaching methodology. Moreover, neither instructors nor students were randomly assigned in most studies. Thus, several competing explanations are possible for any differences between the groups. Finally, the reliability of the handwriting measures used in most studies was not established, jeopardizing the validity of both the assessments and the findings (Graham, 1986a, 1986b).

In order to identify the most salient claims for using a slanted manuscript alphabet, this author examined the claims of various advocates, the available research literature and current handwriting programs. Two basic claims were identified: 1) slanted manuscript makes the transition to cursive writing easier and 2) slanted alphabets are superior because the letters are formed using a single, continuous stroke. Each of these claims is examined in turn.

Claim I: Slanted Manuscript Alphabets Make the Transition to Cursive Writing Easier

The basic claim made by developers and advocates of slanted manuscript letters is that such alphabets do a better job than traditional manuscript in facilitating the transition to cursive writing (McDougal, Littell, 1993; Thurber, 1993b). If this claim is valid, students who learn to print using a slanted manuscript alphabet should become better cursive writers than those who learn to print using traditional manuscript.

Farris (1982) examined this issue in a longitudinal study. At the beginning of the school year, she randomly assigned 86 kindergarten students to two treatment groups. From kindergarten to the first part of 2nd grade, one group was taught slanted manuscript using the D'Nealian program; the other group was taught traditional manuscript using the Zaner-Bloser program. During 2nd grade, each of the two groups made the transition to cursive writing using their respective handwriting programs.

Near the end of 2nd grade, a sample of the students' cursive writing was scored using 15 separate criteria (no information on the reliability of the scores was provided). Overall, students who had been taught traditional manuscript produced more legible cursive writing than students in the D'Nealian group. Students in the D'Nealian group were more likely to misshape cursive letters, extend strokes above and below the guidelines and vary the size of letters. Consequently, in this study the production of cursive writing was not enhanced by D'Nealian instruction.

Similarly, Trap-Porter, Cooper, Hill, Swisher and LaNunziata (1984) compared the cursive writing of 134 1st-grade students who had been taught traditional manuscript using Zaner-Bloser and 112

1st-grade students who had been taught slanted manuscript using D'Nealian. Each student copied the lower-case cursive letters from their respective programs. There were no differences between the two groups of students in the number of cursive letters omitted when copying or, more important, in the number of cursive strokes made correctly. Again, the production of cursive writing was not enhanced by the use of the D'Nealian method.

Finally, in a study by Ourada (1993), 45 3rd-grade students were divided into two groups on the basis of academic skills and behavior. None of the children had previously been taught cursive writing. One of the groups spent four weeks learning to write slanted manuscript letters using the D'Nealian alphabet, followed by eight weeks of cursive writing instruction using the same program. The other group followed the same schedule, but reviewed how to write traditional manuscript letters and learned cursive script using the Zaner-Bloser program.

A cursive writing sample collected at the end of the 12-week instructional period was scored for overall legibility as well as letter formation, slant and size (information on reliability of scores was not provided). Unfortunately, Ourada (1993) did not use statistical procedures to analyze the obtained scores. As a result, this author conducted a series of chi-square analyses to determine if the cursive writing of the two groups differed (see Graham, 1992). He found no differences between the two groups in slant ($X=.94$) or size of cursive letters ($X^2=.38$, df=1). While students in the D'Nealian group were more likely to produce papers with acceptable letter formation ($X^2=4.2$, df=1, $p < .05$), this proved to be a minor distinction. The overall legibility of the papers written by the two groups did not differ significantly ($X^2=.91$, df=1).

Analysis of the available research shows that whether slanted alphabets or more traditional manuscript letters were taught, the resulting quality of children's cursive writing was the same or exhibited only minor and unreliable distinctions. It is possible that slanted manuscript alphabets did not lead to superior cursive writing because they do not facilitate the transition to cursive to the extent claimed. Developers of the D'Nealian (Thurber, 1993a) and McDougal, Littell (1993) handwriting programs have argued that because their manuscript letters are slanted and closely resemble cursive letters, the transition to cursive writing is simple—mainly a matter of adding connecting strokes.

In an analysis of the D'Nealian and McDougal, Littell handwriting programs (Graham, 1992), the author found that almost half (46 percent) of the cursive letters in each program are substantially different from their manuscript counterparts. An additional 21 percent of the cursive letters in D'Nealian and 26 percent of those in the McDougal, Littell program involve small changes in letter formation, such as tightening a curve or shortening a line, in order to add a connecting stroke. While lower-case letters are more constant than upper-case letters, approximately 70 percent of all manuscript letters in either program require some modification for cursive writing beyond simply adding connecting strokes. Consequently, students have to learn not only all of the upper- and lower-case manuscript letters, but a modified or completely different form for most of the cursive letters. Learning cursive writing in these programs is not a simple transition.

It has also been argued that slanted manuscript alphabets facilitate the transition to cursive writing by saving instructional time. For example, Thurber (1983, 1993a) has claimed that D'Nealian cuts in half the time needed to teach cursive. The basis for claims of this nature, however, is unclear. Both the D'Nealian and the McDougal, Littell programs introduce cursive writing one-third of the way through 2nd grade. By the end of the year, all of the upper- and lower-case cursive letters are covered.

> ...the available evidence failed to substantiate the claim that the transition to cursive writing is enhanced by using a slanted manuscript alphabet.

Using the more traditional alphabet, the Zaner-Bloser method provides two options for making the transition to cursive writing. One of the options mirrors the approach taken by D'Nealian and McDougal, Littell: students make the transition to cursive early in 2nd grade and cover all of the cursive letters by the end of the year. With this option, there is no difference in transition time between the two types of manuscript letters. With the second option, cursive writing is introduced in 3rd grade. Although students spend an extra year working on manuscript, the amount of time spent making the transition to cursive is again about one year.

In summary, the available evidence failed to substantiate the claim that the transition to cursive writing is enhanced by using a slanted manuscript alphabet. Programs using either slanted or more traditional manuscript letters produced no reliable differences in children's cursive writing.

Claim 2: Slanted Manuscript Alphabets Use Continuous Strokes To Form Manuscript Letters—Resulting in Better Rhythm, Greater Speed, More Writing and Fewer Reversals Than Traditional Manuscript

Most manuscript letters can be formed by using either a single continuous stroke or two or more basic strokes (e.g., horizontal lines, vertical lines, slant lines, circles, parts of circles). The developers of the two slanted manuscript programs intentionally designed the majority of their manuscript letters so that they could be formed using a single stroke. They claim that this feature of their manuscript alphabet results in writing that is more rhythmical, faster and less directionally confusing.

It must be noted, however, that the continuous stroke method also can be used to form traditional manuscript letters. The Zaner-Bloser program, for example, provides two options for producing manuscript letters. One option involves using four basic strokes to form letters. With this option, the pencil is lifted from the paper when forming three out of every five manuscript letters (e.g., **T, t**). A second option involves using a single stroke to form manuscript letters. With this option, the pencil is lifted from the paper when forming less than half (44 percent) of the manuscript alphabet. In comparison, the pencil is lifted when forming 33 percent of the manuscript letters in the D'Nealian alphabet and 39 percent of the manuscript letters in the McDougal, Littell alphabet.

The differences between continuous stroke manuscript options are even smaller when just lower-case letters are considered. With the D'Nealian and McDougal, Littell programs, only six lower-case letters (**f, i, j, t** and **x**) require a pencil lift. Only two additional letters (**k** and **y**) require a pencil lift with the Zaner-Bloser continuous stroke option. Neither of these letters is particularly common in English words (Zetterson, 1969).

Regardless of the similarities or differences between various handwriting programs, any claims regarding the advantages of a continuous stroke method, for either slanted or traditional manuscript letters, must be considered premature at this point. Beyond testimonials collected by publishers (cf. Coon & Palmer, 1993), no evidence exists that children write more rhythmically, faster or more as a consequence of learning a manuscript alphabet based on continuous stroke letter formation. These claims have simply not been investigated by researchers.

The only issues that have been addressed by researchers involve the effect of continuous stroke letter formation on frequency of reversals and quality of manuscript writing. In a Master's Thesis (Oglesby, 1982) cited by Thurber (1993b), 12 underachieving 2nd-graders were randomly divided into two groups that received nine weeks of manuscript instruction using either the D'Nealian or Zaner-Bloser method. Students assigned to the Zaner-Bloser group used the traditional manuscript alphabet without the continuous stroke option. Every three weeks, the quality of students' manuscript writing (e.g., legibility, letter formation, spacing) was assessed by four teachers (no information on reliability of scores was provided).

Although the overall results of the investigation favored the D'Nealian group, scores on specific handwriting measures were extremely erratic across the three testing sessions (unexplainably going up and down or vice versa).

> ...the letters in the D'Nealian alphabet involve more motions that occur later in children's development.

Therefore, the reliability of the teachers' evaluations, and ultimately the validity of the study, must be questioned.

In the only other study located, Farris (1982) examined the manuscript handwriting performance of 1st-grade students who had used either the D'Nealian or Zaner-Bloser method since kindergarten. Again, students in the Zaner-Bloser group used the traditional manuscript alphabet without the continuous stroke option. Manuscript handwriting samples collected at two points during the year were scored using 15 separate criteria (e.g., letter formation, spacing, slant). No information on the reliability of the scores was provided. Farris found no significant differences between the two groups of students on any of the criteria, including the number of letters reversed.

Farris (1982) may have failed to find an advantage for the D'Nealian manuscript alphabet because slanted and continuous stroke letters may require a greater degree of fine-motor control than the letters in the Zaner-Bloser alphabet without the continuous stroke option. This issue was addressed by Duvall (1985), who assessed the difficulty of the lower-case manuscript letters in these two programs. She found that the letters in the D'Nealian alphabet involve more motions that occur later in children's development, require more retracing of lines and force the hand to change direction more often. In contrast, when using the Zaner-Bloser alphabet without the continuous stroke option the writer has to pay more attention to visual information, such as where strokes begin and meet.

Last, supporters of slanted manuscript alphabets have argued that their continuous stroke letters are especially helpful for students with special needs, reducing frustration and increasing writing fluency (Coon & Palmer, 1993; Jordan, no date; Thurber, 1993b). The author found no scientific evidence, however, to support these claims. As Brown (1993) noted, "No research has been found that would support the use of one system in handwriting over the other in remedial and special education" (p. 68).

Conclusion

A slanted manuscript may not be the best choice for young children for several reasons. First, there is no credible evidence that these alphabets make a difference in children's handwriting. Making the transition to cursive writing does not appear to be enhanced by using a special alphabet like D'Nealian. Similarly, claims that slanted manuscript alphabets are superior because most of their letters are formed with a single, continuous stroke have not been validated.

Second, the use of slanted manuscript alphabets creates several practical problems for teachers. They have to respond to questions from parents who are worried because the new letters do not look "like print" (these alphabets are unusual enough that even the publishers use traditional manuscript in student workbooks). Teachers also have to learn how to write the new letters themselves in order to appropriately model their formation during instruction.

More important, many young children already know how to write to some degree before starting kindergarten or 1st grade. The letters that they learn how to write prior to starting school are, usually, the traditional manuscript. Learning a special alphabet like D'Nealian means that many children would have to relearn letters they can already write. As a result, a "hidden" transition takes place for children who are taught a slanted manuscript alphabet during kindergarten or 1st grade. This transition is also required of children who have been taught traditional print, then transfer to a school using a program such as D'Nealian. Given the lack of supportive evidence and the practical problems involved in implementation, slanted manuscript letters cannot be recommended as a replacement of the traditional manuscript alphabet.

References

Askov, E., & Peck, M. (1982). In H. Mitzel (Ed.), *Encyclopedia of educational research* (pp. 764-766). New York: Free Press.

Brown, V. (1993). D'Nealian handwriting: What it is and how to teach it. In G. Coon & G. Palmer (Eds.), *Handwriting research and information: An administrator's handbook* (pp. 62-71). Glenview, IL: Scott, Foresman.

Coon, G., & Palmer, G. (Eds.). (1993). *Handwriting research and information: An administrator's handbook*. Glenview, IL: Scott, Foresman.

Duvall, B. (1985). Evaluating the difficulty of four handwriting styles used for instruction. *ERS Spectrum, 3,* 13-20.

Early, G. (1973). The case for cursive writing. *Academic Therapy, 9,* 105-108.

Farris, P. (1982). *A comparison of handwriting strategies for primary grade students.* Arlington, VA: ERIC Document Reproduction Service (CS 209 360).

Graham, S. (1986a). A review of handwriting scales and factors that contribute to variability in handwriting scores. *Journal of School Psychology, 24,* 63-72.

Graham, S. (1986b). The reliability, validity, and utility of three handwriting measurement procedures. *Journal of Educational Research, 79,* 373-380.

Graham, S. (1992). Issues in handwriting instruction. *Focus on Exceptional Children, 25,* 1-4.

Graham, S., & Miller, L. (1980). Handwriting research and practice: A unified approach. *Focus on Exceptional Children, 13,* 1-16.

Groff, P. (1964). Who are better writers—The left-handed or the right-handed? *Elementary School Journal, 65,* 92-96.

Hackney, C., & Lucas, V. (1993). *Zaner-Bloser handwriting: A way to self-expression.* Columbus, OH: Zaner-Bloser.

Jordan, D. (no date). *Research: Handwriting issues and special needs.* Glenview, IL: Scott, Foresman.

McDougal, Littell (1993). *Handwriting connections.* Evanston, IL: Author.

Oglesby, B. (1982). *A comparative study of the difference in the manuscript handwriting performance of six below-average second-grade students who experienced the D'Nealian method of handwriting instruction for a nine-week period when compared to six below-average second-grade students who experienced the Zaner-Bloser method of handwriting instruction for a nine-week period, as measured by four judges' scores on a teacher-made checklist.* Unpublished master's thesis, University of North Florida, Jacksonville.

Ourada, E. (1993). Legibility of third-grade handwriting: D'Nealian handwriting versus traditional Zaner-Bloser. In G. Coon & G. Palmer (Eds.), *Handwriting research and information: An administrator's handbook* (pp. 72-87). Glenview, IL: Scott, Foresman.

Templin, E. (1963). The legibility of adult manuscript, cursive, or manuscript-cursive handwriting styles. In V. Herrick (Ed.), *New horizons for handwriting research* (pp. 185-200). Madison, WI: University of Wisconsin Press.

Thurber, D. (1983). *D'Nealian manuscript—An aid to reading development.* Arlington, VA: ERIC Document Reproduction Service (CS 007 057).

Thurber, D. (1993a). *D'Nealian handwriting.* Glenview, IL: Scott, Foresman.

Thurber, D. (1993b). How D'Nealian handwriting meets the needs of all writers. In G. Coon & G. Palmer (Eds.), *Handwriting research and information: An administrator's handbook* (pp. 50-61). Glenview, IL: Scott, Foresman.

Trap-Porter, J., Cooper, J., Hill, D., Swisher, K., & LaNunziata, L. (1984). D'Nealian and Zaner-Bloser manuscript alphabets and initial transition to cursive handwriting. *Journal of Educational Research, 77,* 343-345.

Zettersten, A. (1969). *A statistical study of the graphic system of present-day American English.* Lund, Sweden: Studentlitteratur.

Chapter 3

Paper, pencils, and position:

What is basic in handwriting instruction?

Bil Keane, Inc.
Dist. by King Features Synd.

"It's not penmanship, Grandma.
It's PENCILmanship."

Reprinted with special permission King Features Syndicate.

Introduction

What is basic in handwriting instruction? Because handwriting is a perceptual-motor skill, lessons in handwriting should have a dual purpose. Teachers need to help students learn: 1) how to think about letter formation when they write, and 2) how to position and move their bodies when they write.

During handwriting instruction, students use the same kind of perceptual skills that are important in map-reading. They learn to see that, just as each line on a map represents a feature of the landscape, each unique combination of lines and curves on a page represents a letter of the alphabet. But handwriting is also a motor skill. Like riding a bike, handwriting is learned in part by practicing sequences of body movements until they are locked in "muscle memory." In handwriting, practice makes permanent, so it is important to teach good habits from the start.

The articles in this chapter provide some basic information about what to include in a successful handwriting curriculum. Many of the recommendations are well-supported by research and have long been a part of Zaner-Bloser's approach to handwriting. Fundamentals in five important areas of handwriting instruction are described below.

I. Materials

The materials used for handwriting are less important than the quality of instruction. Choose materials that will support students' development and also motivate them to write.

Writing Instruments

Researchers recommend offering a wide variety of writing instruments in the classroom. Many students choose felt-tip pens or markers as their favorites. These are fun to use, and they promote fluency. Students' selection should also include all types of pencils, pens, crayons, and paintbrushes. Allowing students to use chalk on the chalkboard is an excellent method for handwriting instruction.

Paper

For beginning instruction in manuscript and cursive writing, it is best to use specially lined handwriting paper appropriate for the grade level. The top and bottom guidelines and broken midline help students determine where strokes should meet to form letters with good size and shape. Beginning in the fourth grade, students may use wide-ruled notebook paper for all their written work.

2. Positions for Writing

Whenever students begin a writing task, they need to stop and think about how they are sitting, where the paper is placed on the desk, and how they are holding the pencil. Use the following guidelines.

Sitting Position

Sit back comfortably, bending slightly forward from the waist. Keep feet flat on the floor with one foot slightly in front of the other. Rest both arms comfortably on the desk with the elbows just off the edge.

Paper Position
Manuscript

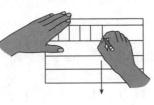

left hand

Place the paper diagonally with the lower right-hand corner pointing a little to the left of the midsection of the body. Pull downstrokes to the left elbow.

right hand

Place the paper square so that the bottom edge is parallel to the desk. Pull downstrokes to the midsection of the body.

Cursive

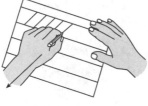
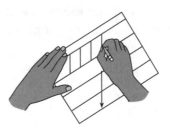

left hand

Place the paper diagonally with the lower right-hand corner pointing a little to the right of the midsection of the body. Pull down-strokes to the left elbow.

right hand

Place the paper diagonally with the lower left-hand corner pointing toward the midsection of the body. Pull downstrokes to the midsection.

Pencil Position

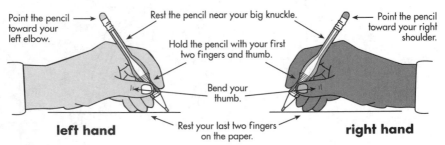

Point the pencil toward your left elbow.

Rest the pencil near your big knuckle.

Point the pencil toward your right shoulder.

Hold the pencil with your first two fingers and thumb.

Bend your thumb.

Rest your last two fingers on the paper.

left hand

right hand

What is basic in handwriting instruction?

3. Basic Strokes

Students will have greater success in handwriting when they recognize that all the letters of the alphabet are formed from the same basic strokes. Identifying and practicing the basic strokes is a prerequisite for learning to write letters.

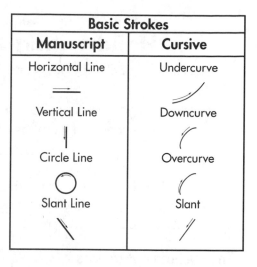

| Basic Strokes | |
Manuscript	Cursive
Horizontal Line	Undercurve
Vertical Line	Downcurve
Circle Line	Overcurve
Slant Line	Slant

4. Modeling and Teaching the Letters

Watching the teacher model letter formation is the best way to learn handwriting. This instruction is enhanced when information about letter formation is provided in three learning modalities. Visual learners can refer to a letter model with numbered arrows. Auditory learners can repeat stroke descriptions after the teacher. Kinesthetic learners can be encouraged to write letters in the air. Asking questions such as "How many slant strokes are in K?" is a good way to help students use their perceptual skills to form a visual-motor image of the letter.

5. Practice

Instruction in forming individual letters should be closely followed by practice in writing words and sentences. Students can maintain the quality of their handwriting with regular practice and self-evaluation. The most effective handwriting practice involves meaningful, real-life tasks such as writing a letter, taking class notes, or filling out a form.

For more information about the basics of handwriting instruction, turn to one of the articles in this chapter. In "Handwriting Instruction," Elinor Ross and Betty Roe present practical, research-based suggestions for teachers. An excerpt from Saskatchewan Education's "Handwriting: A Communication Tool" gives a list of criteria for good handwriting instruction. Finally, Henry Petroski tells the story of the humble pencil and decides that it will never go out of style.

An Excerpt From

Handwriting Instruction

Elinor P. Ross and Betty D. Roe

Teachers must provide direct instruction with supervised practice so that children can learn to write clearly and legibly.

Researchers have been investigating issues related to handwriting instruction. Many of the findings that are of practical value for classroom teachers are presented here.

Instructional Practices

Effective instructional practices for handwriting are related to such factors as the amount of time provided, the materials used, the student's body position, and the classroom environment.

Time Allocation

A major issue that concerns teachers is allotting time for handwriting instruction. Although handwriting occurs while students are engaged in composing and other meaningful writing tasks, many educators feel that periods for direct instruction and supervised practice should be provided regularly. A summary of research indicates that most handwriting lessons last 15 to 20 minutes and occur daily in grades one to four, but only a few times a week in grades five to eight (Askov and Peck, 1982). First-grade teachers spend the most time on handwriting instruction (Addy and Wylie, 1973). Teachers should schedule handwriting lessons on a routine basis, preferably adjacent to other language arts lessons so that skills can be related to reading and writing activities.

Writing Materials

Writing materials are another major consideration in planning handwriting instruction. Primary (large) pencils and regular pencils with soft lead are the most commonly used instruments for handwriting. Writing instruments do not seem to affect legibility, however, so there is no advantage in using primary pencils over using regular pencils (Lamme and Ayris, 1983). Askov and Peck (1982) found that many children preferred using felt-tip pens. In a study they conducted, third graders who wrote with ballpoint or felt-tip pens produced more letters in a story-writing task than did children who wrote with pencils (Askov and Peck, 1982).

> **Wide-lined paper with three guidelines appears to be best for learning both manuscript and cursive writing.**

In general, children need space without many restrictions as they begin to write, so large paper (12 x 18 inches) without lines is good to use with beginning writers. As the children develop finer control of their muscles, the teacher may fold unlined paper along parallel horizontal lines to guide children in the placement of their writing. Paper with wide horizontal lines (with a light line between each pair), either 12 x 18 inches or 9 x 12 inches in size, may be used when children have enough control of space to write between the lines. Wide-lined paper with three guidelines appears to be best for learning both manuscript and cursive writing (Koenke, 1986; Addy and Wylie, 1973). After students have learned to write in cursive, they generally begin using lined notebook paper.

Body Position

The student should sit erectly but comfortably, leaning forward slightly with hips touching the back of the seat and both feet on the floor. The forearms should be resting on the desk at a 45-degree angle to the body, with the elbows just off the desk for easy arm movement. The paper should be parallel with the edge of the desk or at a slight slant for manuscript writing, but it should be slanted for cursive writing. The writer should hold the writing instrument lightly between the thumb and middle finger, about one inch above the point, and let the index finger rest on top of the instrument. The other hand should hold the paper in place and move it slightly as the writing progresses across and down the page.

Classroom Environment

The classroom atmosphere should contribute to learning handwriting skills. Lighting should be adequate, but there should be no glare on work areas. The children should be seated comfortably at seats appropriate for their size so that they can use correct writing posture. Work areas should be uncluttered so that the children are not distracted and have ample room for placing their papers in the correct position. An alphabet strip of the handwriting system being taught should be prominently displayed, preferably at eye level for young children who can then study the letters carefully, trace them with their fingers, and copy them at a close distance. For older children the alphabet strip is usually paced above the chalkboard, so that students can easily refer to the correct forms of the letters while at their desks.... Other samples of correct handwriting should also be visible in the room (i.e., on charts or as labels). The teacher should be encouraging and supportive of children's efforts, realizing that some children will not be able to produce writing as legible as others. At no time should handwriting be used as punishment, because nothing causes handwriting skills to deteriorate as effectively as having students copy sentences a certain number of times.

Instructional Procedures

Teachers must provide direct instruction with supervised practice so that children can learn to write clearly and legibly. When planning instruction, they should keep in mind the objectives of a good handwriting program: to help students (1) develop neat and legible handwriting for purposes of communication, (2) acquire facility in both manuscript and cursive writing so that writers may use either style, (3) gain speed and proficiency in writing, and (4) see the value of good handwriting.

> ...kindergarten children improved most in producing accurate letters when teachers modeled correct letter formation.

Methodology

Researchers have investigated techniques and materials for teaching handwriting in order to find the most effective methods (Peck, Askov, and Fairchild, 1980). The most common strategy for teaching new letters is copying, and researchers have found copying to be superior to tracing. Demonstration along with verbal instruction improves performance in copying, and copying a close model (i.e., on the child's desk) seems to improve performance more than copying a distant model (i.e., from the chalkboard). Other successful strategies are direct instruction in eye-hand coordination, perceptual and motor training, and verbal rule-based instruction. A study by LaNunziata and others (1985) showed that kindergarten children improved most in producing accurate letters when teachers modeled correct letter formation.

Helpful materials and equipment for teaching correct letter formation include transparent overlays, educational television, animated flip books, and programmed workbooks (Askov and Peck, 1982). Computer software can also facilitate handwriting skills by letting students write on the screen with grease pencils and allowing them to compare their letters with models (Furner, 1985).

Sequence of Instruction

Most handwriting instruction follows a sequence similar to that shown below:

1. readiness activities in kindergarten and beginning first grade

2. manuscript writing or printing in first and second grades

3. cursive writing at the end of second grade or beginning of third grade

These time periods should be flexible and should depend primarily on the readiness levels of the students.

Chalkboard Writing

Many educators believe that handwriting instruction should begin at the chalkboard where children have plenty of space, can use large muscles, and can make corrections easily. The teacher should first demonstrate the stroke(s) or letter(s) to be learned and then ask some of the children to practice at the board while others practice at their seats. Not all of the children can work at the board during the same lesson because each child needs adequate space to make free arm movements, but other children can practice at the board during subsequent lessons.

> Many educators believe that handwriting instruction should begin at the chalkboard where children have plenty of space, can use large muscles, and can make corrections easily.

When writing on the board, each child should have a piece of chalk that is at least half size and an eraser that may be held in the hand that is not writing. The chalk should rest lightly on the thumb, with the index finger placed above the chalk and near the writing tip. The children should write at eye level and move their bodies from left to right, keeping pace with their writing as it moves across the board. Using the open space at the board is fine for beginning writers, but children may need to practice placing letters on a line at a later time. By soaking chalk for 20 minutes in sugar water (one part saturated sugar water to three parts water), the teacher can make practice lines that will not erase but will wash off with water.

Lessons in Manuscript

During their readiness activities, children have already been observing and practicing the basic strokes used for handwriting. In order to create interest in making these strokes, the teacher may demonstrate how to make a circle and ask children to make pictures containing circles, such as round pumpkins with jack-o'-lantern faces, doughnuts, bubbles, and lollipops. The teacher should encourage children to think of their own ideas for making other pictures that incorporate the basic strokes, such as a ladder for straight lines and a tent for slanted lines.

When presenting a handwriting lesson, the teacher should follow the procedures given below.

1. Begin each lesson by reminding the children to sit correctly, place paper in the proper position, and hold the pen or pencil correctly.

2. Demonstrate the right way to make letters on the chalkboard. For instance, make all vertical strokes from the top down and all horizontal strokes from left to right.

3. Teach letters containing the easiest strokes first, such as straight lines (l, i, and t).

4. Generally teach letters based on similar strokes together, such as o, b, and e, but avoid teaching letters that are reversals of each other at the same time, such as b and d.

5. Carefully supervise practice by walking among the students. Model the correct way to make a letter at a child's desk if there is a problem.

6. Encourage the children to cross out mistakes rather than erase them because erasing often results in smudged or torn papers.

7. Expect each child to do his or her best work, even though all children may not be capable of meeting handwriting standards. Occasionally return carelessly written papers for recopying so that students will understand that you want good work from them.

Teachers should avoid having beginning writers practice handwriting by copying selections from the chalkboard or a distant chart. Many children lack the eye-hand coordination to transfer what they see in the distance to what they write on paper, and they seem to perform better when the model is close to them, perhaps on each child's desk (Lamme,

What is basic in handwriting instruction?

1979). Even better than having children copy a close-up model is letting them copy their own compositions or experience stories in better form for publication. Copying their own work, especially for an audience, is generally more meaningful than copying someone else's writing.

The teacher may wish to set up a handwriting center with such materials as individual chalkboards with erasers, magic slates, a variety of sizes and shapes of paper, scissors, paste or glue, old magazines, felt-tip pens, crayons, different-sized pencils, samples of manuscript letters, popular easy-reading books, and individual student folders. A folder of each child's work may be kept so that the teacher can observe development of handwriting skill. If able, each child should put his or her name and the date on the paper before beginning to work.

Transition to Cursive Writing

Many children are eager to learn to write in cursive because that is how most adults write. Making the transition from manuscript to cursive requires a great many new skills, however, and should not be treated lightly. As with learning to write in manuscript, students should possess certain readiness skills. They should be able to print reasonably well and they should have a desire to write in cursive. They also need to be able to read cursive writing. The teacher can prepare them for doing this by writing assignments or directions in cursive and reading them aloud from charts or the chalkboard as children observe. Children will need to use fine-muscle control for new movements as they write connected letters with a slant. Practice in making connected loops and upswings can help prepare them for these new demands, but teachers should avoid too much preparation before moving into teaching actual letter formations....

> A folder of each child's work may be kept so that the teacher can observe development of handwriting skill.

Although some educators might argue that some children should start writing in cursive before others, many educators hold that all children should be introduced to cursive writing at the same time. Retaining some children in manuscript while introducing others to cursive places a double burden on the teacher, and children who are not allowed to move with the rest of the class into cursive writing may develop negative attitudes toward handwriting. Also, in a study of 137 third graders, Armitage and Ratzlaff (1985) found little relationship between poor printing and poor cursive writing.

Instructional procedures and lesson plans for teaching cursive writing are similar to those used for teaching manuscript. Some guidelines for teachers to follow when teaching cursive follow.

1. Teach the four basic strokes...used in cursive writing and the vocabulary for them.

2. Begin with the easiest letters, usually **l, i, t,** and **e**. Make them into words, such as *let, tell,* and *little.*

3. Teach new letters in various positions within words so that students understand how they are connected to other letters. For example, when teaching the letter **m**, use it in *mine, time,* and *hum.*

4. Teach lower-case letters first and show connecting strokes.

5. Teach upper-case letters in connection with names, familiar cities and states, days of the week, and months of the year.

6. Demonstrate parallel slant when teaching all letters and words. Possibly use slanted guidelines to help students who are having difficulty.

7. Maintain manuscript skills. Allow children to take spelling tests and write reports in either manuscript or cursive until they become confident in their use of cursive.

References

Addy, Polly, and Richard E. Wylie. "The 'Right' Way to Write." *Childhood Education* 49 (February 1973): 253-254.

Armitage, Doreen, and Harold Ratzlaff. "The Non-Correlation of Printing and Writing Skills." *Journal of Educational Research* 78 (January/February 1985): 174-177.

Askov, Eunice N., and Michaeleen Peck. "Handwriting." In *Encyclopedia of Educational Research.* Vol. 2, 5th ed. New York: Free Press, 1982, pp. 764-766.

Furner, Beatrice A. "Handwriting Instruction for a High-Tech Society: Will Handwriting Be Necessary?" March, 1985. ED 257 119.

Koenke, Karl. "Handwriting Instruction: What Do We Know?" *The Reading Teacher* 40 (November 1986): 214-216.

Lamme, Linda L. "Handwriting in an Early Childhood Curriculum." *Young Children* 35 (November 1979): 20-27.

Lamme, Linda L., and Beulah M. Ayris. "Is the Handwriting of Beginning Writers Influenced by Writing Tools?" *Journal of Research and Development in Education* 17 (Fall 1983): 32-38.

LaNunziata, Louis J., Jr., John O. Cooper, David S. Hill, and Jennifer Trap-Porter. "The Differential Effects of Still Illustration, Motion Illustration, and Modeling on Students' Manuscript Letter Legibility." *Journal of Educational Research* 79 (November/December 1985): 109-113.

Peck, Michaeleen, Eunice N. Askov, and Steven H. Fairchild. "Another Decade of Research in Handwriting: Progress and Prospect in the 1970s." *Journal of Educational Research* 73 (May/June 1980): 283-298.

"Let's mail this postcard to Grandma in an envelope so her letter carrier won't see my handwriting."

An Excerpt From

Handwriting: A Communication Tool

Saskatchewan Education

Beginning writers need regular and guided handwriting practice.

Instruction and Evaluation Suggestions

- Students' first handwriting experiences should be genuine opportunities to express ideas or communicate information to others, not assignments in penmanship.

- Beginning writers need regular and guided handwriting practice.

- Correct sequence of strokes for letter formation as well as proper gripping of writing tools should be modeled and encouraged before inefficient habits form.

- Script models displayed in classrooms and letter formation guidelines should be consistent within a school.

- Script models should be readily accessible to students—at eye level and on desk or table tops rather than above the chalkboard.

- When modeling letter formation for students, verbalize the "steps" and visual cues. Encourage students to repeat the directions aloud so they observe and describe every hand motion.

- Encourage beginning writers to verbalize and "direct" their own letter formation efforts.

- Emphasis on legibility should not interfere with students' personal writing or first drafts.

- Provide a variety of writing tools for children to use for various purposes. Researchers suggest that pencils may be difficult and uninviting tools for beginning writers. Tools that are easier to manipulate and "flow" smoothly across writing surfaces—chalk, markers, crayons—are preferred by many young students.

- Gradually acquaint students with the terminology and components of handwriting which include shape, size, proportion, slant and spacing.

What is basic in handwriting instruction?

- Beginning writers should practice on large surfaces such as chalkboards and charts. This allows larger muscles to be used.

- When demonstrating manuscript or cursive letter formation, group the letters which require similar strokes.

- Efficiency and ease in using manuscript to communicate ideas to others should be interpreted as an indicator of readiness for the transition to cursive writing.

- Opportunities to read material in cursive form should precede the introduction of cursive letter formation.

- Evaluation of handwriting must include students' self-appraisal and awareness of development.

- Compile portfolios of dated writing samples for student, parent, administrator and teacher reference.

- Student-teacher conferences are important for discussion about, and assessment of, handwriting development.

- Teachers and students should collaboratively develop a set of criteria for evaluation. A simple checklist might include questions such as:

  ✓ Are my letters slanting in the same direction?

  ✓ Do my letters sit on the line?

  ✓ Are my lower and upper case letters appropriate in size?

  ✓ Did I leave enough space between letters and words?

  ✓ Is my writing legible? Can others read it?

A Rub-Out?
Why the Pencil Will Survive

Henry Petroski

There are some things, simply, that technology cannot improve on.

The announcement by the Educational Testing Service this week that it plans to replace pencil and paper with computers on its standardized tests prompts a question. Is this:

(a) an end to No. 2 pencils in the exam room?

(b) an end to No. 2 pencils?

(c) an end to all pencils?

(d) none of the above?

The answer—despite the doom and gloom front-page stories in *The New York Times* and *The Washington Post*—is (d). After all, this is not the first time that the sturdy, low-tech pencil has been threatened. Technological advances and materials shortages have written its obituary many times before. And each time, the plucky implement, seemingly on the verge of extinction, left for dead, has bounced back to life.

The modern pencil dates from the middle of the sixteenth century, when a new mineral that made a dark but removable mark was discovered in England's Lake District. The new mineral was called black lead, because it made a blacker line than metallic lead, which had been among the most common means of making a mark on paper without the mess and bother of ink and quill. Black lead also had military applications, especially in casting cannon balls, and so the English mine from which it came was closely guarded and its output regulated. This made the smallest sliver of black lead very costly. Thus the lead, as it had come to be called, was encased in wood not only to keep the fingers clean, but to protect the pricey substance from breaking. The assemblage of lead and wood was called a pencil, after the fine brush known as a *penicillum* that dated back to Roman times.

With the growth of chemical knowledge, pencil lead was found in 1779 to be a form of carbon. It was then given the name graphite, after the Greek word meaning "to write." (The substance that was found so effective in rubbing out pencil marks was called rubber.) When at war with the English in the late eighteenth century, the French could not

What is basic in handwriting instruction?

get pure graphite, and so an engineer named Nicolas-Jacques Conté was assigned the task of coming up with a way of making good pencils out of poor graphite. He found that if he recombined refined graphite with a clay binder, and if he baked the mixture into a ceramic, he could make pencils as good as the renowned English ones. He found, further, that by altering the proportions of graphite and clay, he could make pencils that made lighter and darker marks. Conté used the numbers one, two, etc., to designate different degrees of hardness in his pencils.

Although Henry David Thoreau did not need to take any standardized test to enter college, pencils were instrumental in paying his way through Harvard.

> And each time, the plucky implement...has bounced back to life.

Thoreau's father, John, was an early American pencil-maker, and when Henry David could not keep a teaching job after his graduation in 1837, he worked at the family business, seeking ways to improve the product. He developed the French process to such a degree that by the mid-1840s Thoreau pencils were the best made in America, and Ralph Waldo Emerson bragged that they were made right in Concord. Soon, however, the expanding German pencil firms flooded the American market with their less expensive products, and the Thoreaus were driven out of the pencil business.

By the middle of the nineteenth century, the English source of graphite had been exhausted. At about the same time an equally rich and pure source had been discovered in Asia, and the German firm A.W. Faber gained exclusive rights to it. Soon, Siberian graphite became the world standard for pencils, and other manufacturers began to color their pencils yellow and give them names like Mongol and Mikado to suggest that they too originated in Asia. This influence remains today, with about three out of every four pencils finished in yellow.

From the beginning of pencil-making, the quality of the wood has been as important as that of the graphite, and red cedar from the southeastern United States was long the wood of choice. By the early twentieth century, however, supplies of red cedar became so scarce that pencil-makers bought old barns and fence posts to stay in business. In time, incense cedar from the western United States was found to be a substitute wood, and that is what is most likely to be in a good No. 2 today. Of late, there has been some concern that jelutong, a tropical rain forest tree, is being used increasingly for less expensive pencils. To counter concerns that pencils are wasteful of resources, one company came out with the American EcoWriter pencil, which uses recycled cardboard and newspaper fiber. Perhaps it will be more readily accepted than the plastic variety of some years ago.

The humble wood-case pencil has survived the exhaustion of its earliest and best sources of graphite and red cedar; it has survived the introduction of the mechanical pencil, the fountain pen, the ball-point; it has survived the development of the typewriter and the personal computer (which killed the typewriter); and it will survive the recasting of standardized tests into a new cyber-tech format. There are some things, simply, that technology cannot improve on. Compared to the handy, durable, effective pencil, the mouse is, well, a mouse.

Chapter 4

What is the role of cursive writing today?

CALVIN & HOBBES

Introduction

What is the role of cursive writing today? Reasons for using cursive, or joined writing, have been studied, but not fully understood. Researchers have failed to prove that it is faster to write in cursive than to print. Studies have shown that manuscript is the more legible style. The idea that only a script signature is legally binding is a myth.

So why do we choose to write in cursive, and to teach cursive writing to children? Most adults prefer to use their own personal style of cursive when they write by hand. Many people like the flow of cursive writing—the way that its curves, loops, and rhythmic slant strokes seem to convey our thoughts. Handwriting analysts know that a person's handwriting is as unique as a fingerprint.

Perhaps this opportunity to develop a personal writing style is the reason that so many students are eager to begin "grown-up writing." Learning how to write in cursive is not an absolute necessity, but it is a rite of passage in our culture. One important reason for teaching cursive is that children want to learn it!

Most schools begin teaching cursive in the second or third grade. In the intermediate and middle school years, a common problem is that students do not get the instruction and practice necessary for maintaining their cursive skills. Upper-grade teachers, faced with stacks of sloppy and illegible student papers, often suffer the most in the absence of consistent, school-wide handwriting instruction.

In deciding what to include in cursive handwriting instruction, schools should consider the following recommendations.

Make sure students are ready to begin cursive.

Before they learn to write in cursive, students should be able to: 1) write legibly in manuscript, 2) recognize cursive letters, 3) read cursive writing, and 4) demonstrate an understanding of cursive slant. Encouraging students to master manuscript writing in grades K–2 will help build a strong foundation for cursive instruction.

Make an informed choice about when to begin cursive.

Zaner-Bloser materials offer a choice for beginning cursive either in Grade 2 or Grade 3. It is important to know that cursive is a new skill that requires time to introduce and teach, regardless of promises made by italic-style programs such as D'Nealian. Transition time is not reduced by these programs, nor is the quality of students' cursive improved. Because manuscript writing is a lifelong skill, it should continue to be emphasized. Electing to begin cursive in Grade 3 has the advantage of allowing students to use manuscript extensively for creative writing during Grade 2.

Emphasize legibility and speed.

Expect and value legible writing in all subjects. Discuss consequences of illegibilities, such as sloppily written words that can look like misspellings. Help students increase speed by combining handwriting lessons with real writing tasks such as note-taking.

Teach corrective strategies to older students.

It's never too late for students to improve their handwriting. Short lessons for older students should focus on corrective strategies for common problems. Students will show more awareness of the quality of their handwriting when they know that a looped cursive i can look like e, or that some letter-to-letter joinings can be tricky.

The articles in this chapter discuss issues surrounding cursive handwriting today. In "They Can't Write!" professor Edward Ericson considers his students' reluctance to write in cursive and wishes they had been taught this important skill as children. News articles from Chicago and Florence, Oregon, report that cursive writing continues to be a useful means of communication for students, despite widespread computer use. Finally, a research study finds that, when it comes to learning cursive, students who learn D'Nealian manuscript have no advantage over those who use vertical manuscript.

Zaner-Bloser Cursive

They Can't Write!

Edward E. Ericson, Jr.

Only too late will children discover which
basic tools they have been deprived of.

Students today can't write. No, I don't mean they can't string words together into sentences and string sentences together into paragraphs. That's old news.

I mean they can't write. I mean cursive, handwriting, penmanship—that little skill kids used to learn in the second and third grades, as soon as their motor skills developed. Never mind the art of effectively moving a significant thought from one head to another by means of little black marks on white paper. Kids today can't string letters together into words. They can't form ovals, loops, and humps. They don't know how to get from an **o** to an **s** or an **r** without lifting the pencil off the paper. I hope Mistah Palmer—he of the Method—is dead.

Until recently, I had dismissed my students' intimations of their scribbling inadequacy. Then a *New York Times* writer penned an article on the subject. Only at that point did I realize my students had meant what they said: They felt humiliated and betrayed for a deficiency not of their own making.

> They don't know how to get from an **o** to an **s** or an **r** without lifting the pencil off the paper.

Now, for years I have resisted my colleagues' laments about the decline in our students' preparedness. We're just getting old and grumpy, I thought. Alas, I must concede that my students' eager faces deceived me into wishful thinking. I had long admitted that freshman composition is a remedial exercise since, in theory, students should already be able to put their thoughts into written form before entering an institution ostensibly devoted to higher learning. But certain compromises with reality must always be made.

As for cursive, in my naiveté I assumed that students who used printed letters for their essay exams were simply seeking maximum legibility. Then at one final exam my casual mention of cursive caused a student momentary panic for fear that I might be going to require it.

She wrote a relieved addendum in cursive, and I could understand from her labored, childlike scrawl why she doubted she could generate 800 to 1,000 words in the three-hour period.

Now I am wondering—this is unbearable—if I should use the early periods of my composition course to teach cursive! Remediation is one thing. But doing in the thirteenth year what wasn't done in the second and third years? Early retirement starts to look really, really good.

When I consulted a colleague in the Education Department, she confirmed my worst fears. Teachers say they are asked to do too many new things, she explained (I didn't want to know what), and so some old things must go. There are supposedly diminishing returns in teaching cursive in the computer age. So in the name of being practical, we turn minimalist. Only too late will children discover which basic tools they have been deprived of.

Products of our schools, in other words, may soon not be able to sign their names. On their personal checks they may give a whole new meaning to the concept of Generation X.

PEANUTS

PEANUTS reprinted by permission of United Feature Syndicate, Inc.

Handwriting Goes With the Flow

Stephen Lee, *Chicago Tribune*

In the age of e-mail, handwriting methods are adapting
to the times, becoming less fancy, but,
to use computer language, more user-friendly.

In the 19th Century, teachers regularly debated the precise angle
that one should hold a pen to create the most pleasing cursive writing.
Penmanship was considered not only an essential skill of everyday life
but a small barometer of breeding and character.

Certainly John Hancock would have made an impression on the
Declaration of Independence with the size of his signature, but perhaps
not his indelible mark on history were it not for the flourish of that J
and H.

But since the early 20th Century, a host of factors—including
budget cuts, curriculum changes and cultural influences—have gradually
come to challenge the time-honored art of handwriting in schools. And
now, in the last decade or so, the computer has accelerated the demise as
kids as young as kindergarten age learn to write on electronic keyboards.

Meanwhile, handwriting has gone from being a separate subject to
something usually covered only in 3rd grade and then folded into other
subjects. Once taught by specially trained experts whose own penmanship was considered sterling, handwriting often is learned through
handouts and the alphabet cards above the chalkboard.

The result is that some pupils are reaching junior high school with
handwriting that is virtually illegible, teachers say, a hodgepodge of
styles that scarcely conforms to any accepted method.

All of this has made some education officials wonder whether, in a
world in which handwritten letters are fading and most business is conducted electronically, the next step of evolution is for cursive writing to
be phased out in favor of printing—or "manuscript," as it is known—
and the keyboard. Some even question whether handwriting will be
taught everywhere in 10 years.

"Except for your signature on a check, we don't need cursive. You
can certainly print as legibly or even more legibly," said Karl Koenke, an
associate education professor at the University of Illinois at Urbana-
Champaign. "We now have three things in the curriculum: printing,

What is the role of cursive writing today?

cursive and keyboard. If I were going to eliminate something, I would eliminate cursive."

Yet other education experts, while admitting that good handwriting is not as critical as it once was, are taking steps to make sure that it does not get left in the dust of the Information Superhighway. And handwriting methods are adapting to the times, becoming less fancy but, to use computer language, more user-friendly.

"Handwriting has taken a big beating because of computers and keyboards," sighed Donald Thurber, a Michigan teacher who created the popular D'Nealian method of manuscript and cursive writing in the late 1970s.

He might be heartened by the scene in Elizabeth Taglieri's 3rd-grade class in Lake Zurich. Pupils learn how to use the computer one morning a week, and many think typing up their papers is easier than writing them out by hand.

> "Computers are great, but there's always going to be a need for handwriting."

But every other morning, they still pull out their chewed-up No. 2 pencils, hunch over their desks and copy down words and sentences in their best cursive handwriting.

"Computers are great, but there's always going to be a need for handwriting," said Taglieri, a teacher at the Whitney Elementary School.

Garvey Elementary School on Chicago's South Side adopted a new cursive handwriting program last fall after teachers became distressed that pupils were learning the former method so poorly that they were making up their own ways of writing by the 6th grade.

Hibbard Elementary School on Chicago's Northwest Side did the same thing three years ago, and Principal Anthony Jelinek regularly checks pupils' work for poor letter formation.

Since the late 1980s, Aldon-Hebron Elementary School District 19 in McHenry County has extended its handwriting drills all the way to 8th grade and even has all teachers take handwriting training sessions each year.

Other districts, such as Buffalo Grove's Kildeer Elementary School District 96, are re-examining their programs to guarantee cursive handwriting's place in the curriculum.

Some Catholic schools even send their pupils' samples to a Hebron penmanship instructor for regular checkups.

At the same time, most major cursive systems are becoming faster to learn and are losing the traditional flourishes and loops to get down to what might be considered fighting weight: faster, simpler, better able to keep up with keyboards and printers.

"We've changed with the times, knowing that people don't have time for a lot of flourishes," said Richard Northup of the Columbus, Ohio-based Zaner-Bloser Co., which revised its alphabet last year. "Teachers really did want it simpler."

Purists scoff at these modern alphabets and methods, but the history of cursive handwriting has been one of seeking faster and arguably more legible methods of communicating on paper.

The Spencerian method dominated the late 19th Century with its rigid posture and ornate characters because it was faster. It was replaced for the same reason by the business-writing method of A.N. Palmer, whose company had its last headquarters in Schaumburg before it was bought and closed in the late 1980s.

Handwritten letters have lost ground to phone calls, word-processed documents, faxes and electronic mail. Keyboards and shorthand make up many adults' experience with the written word rather than the cursive they once learned, and they either print or type when they want to ensure legibility. There may be more and more written communication and information, but it's done less and less in cursive.

Meanwhile, pupils begin learning how to type even as they learn how to print in 1st grade. When they do write by hand in class or at home, they are usually required to do it in cursive after the 3rd grade, but they also are producing more and more drafts and final papers on their home computers or in the school library.

"We place such an emphasis on reading and math that this was something that was pushed aside. Handwriting really took a back seat," said Garvey Principal Patricia Taylor. "It was being taught by giving students a worksheet, when years ago we actually did the air writing and more of that kind of thing which was actually needed."

> **[Cursive] is still viewed by teachers and pupils as a sign of maturity and a necessary part of developing and expressing one's style and personality.**

Tradition, perhaps more than anything, has kept cursive handwriting a part of the elementary school curriculum. It is still viewed by teachers and pupils as a sign of maturity and a necessary part of developing and expressing one's style and personality.

What is the role of cursive writing today?

It also is allegedly faster than printing and more personal and attractive than word processing, teachers and handwriting experts say. There also are more standardized achievement and admissions tests requiring a handwritten essay, a development that should scare some students into more legible handwriting.

> There...are more standardized achievement and admissions tests requiring a handwritten essay, a development that should scare some students into more legible handwriting.

Lake Zurich 3rd grader Samantha Cooper, 8, offered another common reason: "You might not have a computer all the time."

These reasons do not necessarily guarantee cursive's long-term place in the curriculum but should help keep it around, some teachers say.

"We haven't been able to switch to the metric system. I don't think we're going to switch out of cursive writing," said Eunice Askov, an education professor at Penn State University who has studied handwriting trends.

And no matter what some adults may think when remembering their experiences learning to connect the letters and trying to decipher their cursive now, that suits some children fine.

"First we hated doing it. Now we're getting used to it, so it's easy," said James Weinman, 9, a 3rd grader at Ravenswood School on Chicago's North Side who said he also used to hate his teacher when she started teaching cursive. "It helps me flow, and it feels smooth. It's like a roller coaster."

"It's pretty easy reading the computer," said Remi Farina, 8, of Lake Zurich, "but some writing is neat enough that you can read it by itself."

Schools Promote Handwritten Letters

Siuslaw News, Florence, OR

...an alarming number of students cannot write cursive by the time they reach middle school.

———————————

Handwritten letters and notes in cards that are mailed in a stamped envelope—and not e-mailed—are making a comeback, according to the U.S. Department of Education.

The problem is, it takes time to make a letter or address a card for an occasion such as Mother's Day.

But most moms think it's well worth it, given the happiness it brings when going to the mailbox in anticipation of receiving something private, something personal, something addressed just to them.

An informal survey of mothers in Florence—who have sons, daughters or grandchildren living elsewhere—found almost all of them saying they treasure something handwritten over a computerized greeting.

Kate Morris, a regular at the Florence Senior Booster Center, says she keeps all her children's letters. Morris and others say that receiving an e-mail is just not the same.

By contrast, letter-writing has always meant something special. Hallmark greeting card commercials also focus on the many human emotions that go into sending wishes via the traditional mailbox.

Although schools have been among the first to seize changes wrought by the Internet—which shattered linear handwriting—there's a movement afoot to make sure students can compose handwritten letters.

A stream of books and pamphlets produced from data researched by the U.S. Department of Education, and from several recent university studies, shows that an alarming number of students cannot write cursive by the time they reach middle school.

Studies point to students being able to "keyboard" before they can master cursive letter or report writing.

The Department of Education predicts that as computers gain even more influence in the classroom, things every student is presumed to know—such as handwriting—will suffer.

Because handwriting, and not just printing or knowing how to keyboard, is considered a critical measure of student success, the Department of Education has launched a country-wide initiative to

What is the role of cursive writing today?

have students in the elementary school grades of third to sixth writing handwritten letters and papers.

Although this initiative has not yet become part of the curriculum in schools here, Mary Carlisle at Rhododendron Primary School says there's a plan to adopt it at the elementary school.

In turn, a spokesperson at the elementary school said it will probably start with third-graders. But at this time "it's in the middle of a committee who are researching this new writing program."

Karen Perry, an eighth-grade language arts teacher at Siuslaw Middle School, said in an interview this week that any basic handwriting program should start at the elementary level.

"We expect them to have good handwriting skills when they get to the middle school level," Perry added.

As part of the Oregon Educational Act for the 21st Century—a series of educational standards intended to prepare children for life in the 21st century—the handwriting program will be graded during a yearly assessment by the state of Oregon.

Performance standards will be measured with state writing tests given over the course of three consecutive days, according to criteria developed by the Oregon Department of Education.

The writing tests are designed for students in grades three, five, eight, and 10. The tests will assess students' ability in the areas of developing their own ideas (without a computer), sentence fluency and spelling, grammar and punctuation.

E-mail doesn't give one the thrill of tearing open that envelope, its flap gummed with the sender's tongue; withdrawing that piece of paper and seeing that aged, quaint, tender salutation, "Dear Mother."

D'Nealian and Zaner-Bloser Manuscript Alphabets and Initial Transition to Cursive Handwriting

Jennifer Trap-Porter, John O. Cooper,
David S. Hill, and Karen Swisher: The Ohio State University
Louis J. LaNunziata: University of North Carolina, Wilmington

This study compared cursive handwriting samples from II2 first graders who had received instruction using the new alphabet and I34 first-grade students who were instructed using traditional manuscript forms. The two groups did not differ in production of cursive letters.

Traditionally, manuscript handwriting instruction has preceded instruction in cursive handwriting. Proponents of this approach suggest that the manuscript letter strokes are easier to perform than cursive strokes for kindergarten and first-grade students. The similarity between the manuscript letters and reading materials is considered an advantage for beginning readers and writers (Huitt, 1972).

The practice of progressing from manuscript to cursive strokes is not without opposition. Early (1976) found that exclusive use of cursive writing did not impair initial progress in reading or spelling. His results suggested that instruction in two alphabets was unwarranted. Lehaman (1980) argued that manuscript strokes are not easier to initiate than cursive forms. Further, he contended that the use of manuscript writing may lead to frustration if students are given the impression that they should stop manuscript writing and learn "real" handwriting.

Recently, a new manuscript alphabet, the D'Nealian Manuscript (Scott, Foresman & Company, 1978), was developed. D'Nealian manuscript letters are written with a slant and show more resemblance to the cursive letters than do traditional manuscript alphabets. Most D'Nealian manuscript letters are formed with one continuous stroke.

Though materials used for sales promotion of the D'Nealian manuscript alphabet state that the program will facilitate transition between manuscript and cursive writing (Scott, Foresman & Company, 1982, p. 1), data are not available to support this claim. The purpose of this study was to test the effect of training under two manuscript alphabets, D'Nealian and Zaner-Bloser, on first graders' initial attempts at producing cursive letters.

Method

Eleven classes of first graders attending six schools in central Ohio served as subjects. Classes were selected using the following criteria:

1. an expressed interest, and cooperation, of both principals and teachers;

2. formal handwriting instruction only in manuscript letters had been given to students; and

3. previous training in writing the D'Nealian Manuscript Alphabet or the Zaner-Bloser Manuscript Alphabet (1976) had occurred.

One group of subjects came from five classrooms in which students were taught manuscript handwriting using the D'Nealian Alphabet. Class size ranged from 15 to 31 students. Of the total 112 students in these classes, 60 were girls and 52 were boys. The other group of subjects consisted of students who were taught manuscript handwriting using the Zaner-Bloser Alphabet. Class size ranged from 18 to 33 students. Of the 134 students, 69 were boys and 65 were girls.

Setting

Students worked at their desks or tables in their classrooms. The work surface was clear except for the students' writing materials.

Materials

Subjects used one training sheet of the 26 lowercase cursive letters developed from the Zaner-Bloser Creative Growth Transitional Cursive Alphabet (1976). The letters, constructed with a line weight of one millimeter, were printed on paper with sets of parallel lines. The spaces between the headline and midline, midline and baseline, and descender space below the baseline were seven-sixteenths of an inch (1.11 centimeters). Since there were no major differences between the Zaner-Bloser and the D'Nealian cursive alphabets, the same model letter sheet was used with all subjects.

Copy Paper

Writing paper Number Two published by the Zaner-Bloser Handwriting Company was used. Spacing between the lines was seven-sixteenths of an inch (1.11 centimeters). The paper measured 8½ inches (21.59 centimeters) by 11 inches (27.94 centimeters) and contained red and green parallel lines.

Evaluative Overlay

Trap-Porter, Gladden, Hill, and Cooper (1983) designed a set of overlays to measure one-millimeter deviations of student letter samples from model letters. Using the overlays, individual letter strokes are evaluated based on slant, length, containment within boundaries on the overlay, contact with other strokes, and closed circular strokes. (See Trap et al. [1983] for a complete description of the evaluation criteria and scoring procedure.)

Procedures

The experimenter began the session with verbal interaction designed to help students feel at ease. Students were then given one sheet of model letters, one sheet of copy paper, and one standard number two pencil. Students were told to write their names on the paper and then put their pencils down. When all students had finished writing their names, the experimenter asked the students if they had ever seen letters like those on the model letter sheet. The experimenter briefly discussed manuscript and cursive forms of writing.

Specifically, the experimenter pointed out that each cursive letter is written without stopping or lifting the pencil except to dot the **i** or **j** or to cross the **x** and **t**. The experimenter also stressed that the cursive letters are slanted and that the copy paper should be slanted when writing cursive letters. The experimenter pointed out that all letters sit on the red line (baseline) and that most strokes begin and end on either the red line or the blue line above the red line. The experimenter then drew lines on the chalkboard. Students were asked to figure out how to write each letter. The experimenter explained the numbers and arrows on the model letter sheet and demonstrated how to write the letter **a**. After any student questions were answered, the experimenter told the students to copy the letters from the model letter sheet on their copy paper. Students were told to try to make each letter look just like it did on the model letter sheet: the same size and shape. Students were then told to pick up their pencil and begin.

Student behavior such as listening, working, putting pencils down, and watching were praised. At no time did any student receive any feedback on the quality or correctness of his or her writing sample. When students had finished copying the letters, the copy papers, model letter sheets, and pencils were collected. Students were thanked for working and the experimenter left the room. The total session lasted between 20 and 30 minutes for each classroom.

Interscorer agreement

Two scorers were trained to assess the writing samples for letter strokes meeting criteria by using the evaluative overlays and procedures developed by Trap et al. (1983). The scorers practiced until a minimum of 85% agreement was met, then scoring of the samples began. The first scorer evaluated all 246 samples. Using a table of random numbers, 74 samples were selected for blind interobserver agreement checks. The second scorer was not involved in the study beyond the independent checking of samples. The second scorer did not know the purpose of the study or the difference in the groups. Percentage of agreement was calculated for each sample by dividing the number of agreements between observers by the number of agreements plus disagreements, and multiplying by 100.

The percentage of agreement on total strokes ranged from 81 to 100 with a mean of 93.3%. The percentage of agreement on the 39 Zaner-Bloser-trained students' samples ranged from 86 to 100% with a mean of 94.2%. The percentage of agreement on the 35 D'Nealian-trained students' samples ranged from 81 to 98% with a mean of 92.3%.

Results

The number of correct strokes made by each student was analyzed. For the group receiving training with Zaner-Bloser materials the average percentage of correct cursive strokes was 73.49% for males and 72.86% for females. The male and female students in the D'Nealian group averaged 72.81% and 72.40% correct cursive strokes, respectively.

The data were analyzed to determine whether there were significant differences between groups in the number of letters omitted during the copying task. Fifty students (37.3%) in the Zaner-Bloser group omitted letters. The difference was not significant ($x^2 = 0.37$; $df = 1$; $p = 7.05$).

An analysis of variance was performed to determine the type of instruction (Zaner-Bloser and D'Nealian) and sex differences in number of correct cursive strokes made. The results of the ANOVA are reported in Table 1. The results indicated no significant type of instruction ($F = 0.78$; $df = 1,242$; $p = 7.05$) or gender difference ($F = 0.78$; $df = 1,242$; $p = 7.05$). The type by sex interaction was not significant ($F = 0.03$; $df = 1,242$; $p = 7.05$).

TABLE I. ANOVA Summary

Source	SS	df	ms	F	p
Type of instruction	19.59	1	19.59	0.90	7.05
Sex	16.68	1	16.68	0.78	7.05
Type × sex	0.70	1	0.70	0.03	7.05
Error	5255.02	242	21.72		

Discussion

The results of this study suggest that first graders' production of cursive letters was not enhanced by instruction employing D'Nealian manuscript instructional materials. There was no difference in the number of cursive letter strokes at criteria by students who had received either Zaner-Bloser or D'Nealian instruction in manuscript letter writing.

Several factors should be considered in interpreting these results. First, the actual instruction by the first-grade teachers using the two sets of materials was not controlled. The equality of performance between the two groups may have been due to the teacher's varying from prescribed use of the materials. Second, students receiving D'Nealian instruction use writing paper with normal space-size. This study required the students to copy cursive letters on wide spaced transition writing paper. Space-size of writing paper may have affected the performance of the D'Nealian group. Third, the publishers of the D'Nealian materials suggest that students who receive D'Nealian instruction may learn cursive strokes more quickly when cursive writing instruction is given in later grades. This study did not address that possibility. Future research should consider instruction, space-size of writing paper, and the effect of instruction in early grades on the ease of acquisition of cursive strokes for older students in investigating the utility of the D'Nealian manuscript writing instructional materials.

> The results of this study suggest that first graders' production of cursive letters was not enhanced by instruction employing D'Nealian manuscript instructional materials.

References

Early, G. H. Handwriting, reading, and cursive spelling achievement. *Academic Therapy*, 1976, *12*, 67-74.

Huitt, R. Handwriting: the state of the craft. *Childhood Education*, 1972, *48*, 219-223.

Lehaman, C. Teaching and learning the craft of handwriting. *The Education Digest*, 1980, *45*, 50.

Scott, Foresman & Company. *Research and information: Handwriting research and D'Nealian handwriting methods—an update.* Chicago: Author, 1982.

Scott, Foresman & Company. *Teaching handwriting: A conversation with Donald N. Thurber.* Chicago: Author, not dated.

Scott, Foresman & Company. *D'Nealian manuscript alphabet.* Chicago: Author, 1978.

Trap-Porter, J., Gladden M. A., Hill, D. S., & Cooper, J. O. Space-size and accuracy of second- and third-grade students' cursive handwriting. *Journal of Educational Research*, 1983, *76*, 231-234.

Zaner-Bloser Company. *Creative growth manuscript alphabet.* Columbus, OH: Author, 1976. (a)

Zaner-Bloser Company. *Creative growth traditional cursive alphabet.* Columbus, OH: Author, 1976. (b)

"That's printing and this is cursive
writing. In cursive all the
letters hold hands."

Reprinted with special permission of King Features Syndicate.

Chapter 5

Handwriting and the writing process:
How does handwriting support proficient writers?

"Mommy! Billy's writing with the mustard!"

Reprinted with special permission of King Features Syndicate.

Introduction

How does handwriting support proficient writers? Over the past twenty-five years, steady interest in the writing process and in the qualities of good writing has resulted in profound changes in the way we teach students to write. Students today are asked to write more, and write well. We expect them to master the writing process, and to demonstrate their proficiency on a variety of district and statewide tests. Faced with these high expectations for writing instruction, it is no surprise that educators have renewed interest in one of the most critical support skills for writing—handwriting.

Like spelling and grammar, handwriting is a subskill of the complex task of writing. Competent, legible handwriting is part of the "equipment" students need before they set out on the journey of writing an essay or a story. In his book *A Fresh Look at Writing*, Donald Graves explains:

> When the handwriting flows, the writer has better access to his own thoughts and information. This is why writers want to write. This is why handwriting is for writing. (1994)

The research articles in this chapter take a closer look at the work of student writers who have the benefit of this "flow" of good handwriting, and those who don't. They conclude that handwriting skills do play a significant role in students' ability to become proficient writers.

In addition to helping individual students with the composing process, legible handwriting improves communication in the classroom and benefits all members of a writing community. The suggestions that follow show how handwriting can be emphasized within a writing curriculum.

Encourage students to practice good handwriting until it is automatic.

When students are writing, they shouldn't have to interrupt their thought process to remember how to form **f**, or to make sure they join **o** and **r** correctly. Provide good handwriting models in the classroom and make time for regular practice. Automatic handwriting allows students to devote their full concentration to the content of their writing.

Banish the "sloppy copy."

While it's true that a student's best handwriting is required only for the publishing stage of the writing process, illegible writing is never okay. The term "sloppy copy" invites careless handwriting. Teach students that legible notes and drafts aid revision and show courtesy to teachers and writing partners.

Ask students to evaluate handwriting during the editing stage of the writing process.

Poor handwriting can distract readers and interfere with the message students want their writing to send. Have students locate illegible passages in their writing at the same time they check for misspellings and grammatical errors. Teach students how to evaluate and improve their handwriting.

Coach students to use good handwriting for testing.

Studies show that test evaluators award higher scores to responses written with good handwriting. Evaluators even show a preference for neatly handwritten answers over word-processed writing. Many readers feel a greater sense of a writer's "voice" and a stronger personal connection to the writer when a piece is handwritten. Let students know that handwriting matters on tests.

The articles in this chapter uncover evidence of the importance of good handwriting to student writers. First, Bond reports on a University of Washington study demonstrating that both composition and handwriting improve when the two skills are taught together. A University of Maryland study by researchers Graham, Harris, and Fink shows that failure to develop handwriting skills in the early grades may lead to arrested writing development. Next, research by Jones and Christensen finds that 53% of the variance in story-writing scores for a group of first graders can be accounted for by the students' ability to write letters. Finally, Roblyer reviews several research articles concluding that students get higher scores on tests when they write their essays by hand.

Handwriting Instruction: Key to Good Writing

Cheryl Murfin Bond

The mental processes involved in handwriting, experts point out, are connected to other important learning functions, such as storing information in memory, retrieving information, manipulating letters, and linking them to sound when spelling.

Good handwriting and the ability to write strong compositions, it turns out, go hand in hand. That's what a study of Seattle first-graders revealed to researchers at the University of Washington and University of Maryland. The study's findings and related research at other institutions across the nation lend weight to theories linking poor handwriting skills in young children to learning disabilities in older kids.

> **Good handwriting and the ability to write strong compositions, it turns out, go hand in hand.**

"Older students who have done poorly from the beginning come to think of themselves as not being writers, so they don't like writing and avoid it," UW professor of education Virginia Berninger said in a summary of the ongoing research funded by the National Institute for Child Health and Human Development. "As a result, their higher-level composing skills don't get developed. We think that if we intervene early with handwriting and spelling instruction, we can prevent problems with written expression later."

The handwriting study directed by Berninger and UW professor Robert Abbott is the first substantial study pointing to handwriting as a possible indicator of "disgraphia," or substantial writing disability, says Shirley Cramer, director of the national Coordinated Campaign for Learning Disabilities. Looking for such red flags early in a child's life—as early as kindergarten and first grade—may allow more kids to benefit from early intervention.

"It's the first indicator of the importance of early intervention for kids in the area of handwriting," says Cramer. "They are giving us some good benchmarks, pointing us to signs of kids who may need extra help.

How does handwriting support proficient writers?

The earlier you intervene, the better chance a child has of success in school. We think it's important that people know that [poor handwriting] is in the mix" as a possible indicator of future learning problems. The mental processes involved in handwriting, experts point out, are connected to other important learning functions, such as storing information in memory, retrieving information, manipulating letters, and linking them to sound when spelling.

The research conducted at the University of Washington supports the researchers' position that the mechanical process of handwriting should be taught in tandem with the more creative process of composition. When the two are taught together, UW researchers say, skills in both areas improve more readily than when handwriting and composition are taught at different times of the day or week.

"Handwriting should not be taught just for the sake of teaching handwriting as an isolated skill," says Berninger. "It should be taught as a tool for written communication. Every time a child practices letter formation as warm-up, they should be given the opportunity to compose and use the tool for a purpose."

Ironically, the discovery that handwriting and composition work together to improve a child's written communication abilities comes at a time when computers are more prevalent in schools and handwriting instruction has been de-emphasized.

"What this tells me is that you can't abandon the handwriting piece," says Cramer. "Just because we all have computers now, we just can't ignore handwriting, especially given this research that shows it's attached to so many other mental-growth processes. We are thrilled to have researchers making these connections."

A Handwriting Method

Is there a key to handwriting success among first-grade students? Berninger and Abbott found that at least one approach used in their most recent study appeared to help students master handwriting more easily than other instruction methods. Children who were asked to study a letter marked with directional arrows showing how to form the letter had a much easier time recalling and

> If the formation of letters becomes automatic, the child has more mental resources available to think about what to say and how to say it during composing.

then duplicating the letter on paper. During the study, students were also directed to practice all 26 letters in 20-minute tutoring sessions, writing each letter only one to three times. This approach to instruction, which differs from the traditional method of copying several rows of a single letter before moving to another letter, resulted in children making letters more accurately and automatically. Instant letter recall leads to better writing, researchers believe.

"If the formation of letters becomes automatic, the child has more mental resources available to think about what to say and how to say it during composing," explains Berninger.

PEANUTS reprinted by permission of United Feature Syndicate, Inc.

How does handwriting support proficient writers?

Excerpts From

Is Handwriting Causally Related to Learning to Write? Treatment of Handwriting Problems in Beginning Writers

Steve Graham,
Karen R. Harris, and Barbara Fink:
University of Maryland

These findings indicate that handwriting is causally related to writing, and that explicit and supplemental handwriting instruction is an important element in preventing writing difficulties in the primary grades.

The contribution of handwriting on learning to write was examined in an experimental training study involving beginning writers with and without an identified disability. First grade children, experiencing handwriting and writing difficulties, participated in 27, 15-minute sessions designed to improve the accuracy and fluency of their handwriting. In comparison to their peers in a contact control condition receiving instruction in phonological awareness, students in the handwriting condition made greater gains in handwriting as well as compositional fluency immediately following instruction and six months later. The effects of instruction were similar for students with and without an identified disability. These findings indicate that handwriting is causally related to writing, and that explicit and supplemental handwriting instruction is an important element in preventing writing difficulties in the primary grades.

Horace Greeley, the founder of the *New Yorker*, often wrote notes and letters that were difficult to decipher. After writing a letter, indicating that he would be unavailable to make a solicited presentation, he received a reply, noting that it took some time to translate his response, but that his requested date, terms, and honorarium were acceptable (Hendrickson, 1994).

Unfortunately, misinterpretations are not the only consequence of handwriting difficulties. For children, there are at least three additional unwanted results. One, poor penmanship may influence perceptions about a child's competence as a writer. When teachers or other adults are asked to evaluate two or more versions of a paper differing only in handwriting quality, neatly written papers are assigned higher marks for writing quality than papers of poorer legibility (e.g., Briggs, 1980; Chase, 1986; Hughes, Keeling, & Tuck, 1983). Two, difficulties with handwriting can interfere with the execution of composing processes during the act of writing (Graham, 1990; Scardamalia, Bereiter, & Goleman, 1982). Having to consciously attend to handwriting processes while composing may tax the writer's processing memory (see Berninger, 1999), interfering with other writing processes, such as content generation and planning. For instance, having to switch attention during composing to mechanical demands, such as having to think about how to form a particular letter, may lead the writer to forget ideas or plans already held in working memory. Third, and most important to the current study, handwriting difficulties

> ...difficulties mastering handwriting skills may lead young children to avoid writing and develop a mind set that they cannot write....

may constrain a child's development as a writer. As Berninger, Mizokawa, and Bragg (1991) noted, difficulties mastering handwriting skills may lead young children to avoid writing and develop a mind set that they cannot write, resulting in arrested writing development. In addition, handwriting may require so much effort for some young writers that they develop an approach to composing (i.e., knowledge telling) that minimizes the use of other writing processes, such as planning and revising, because they exert considerable processing demands as well (McCutchen, 1996).

◆ ◆ ◆

In the present study, we examined the impact of supplementary handwriting instruction on the handwriting and writing performance of first grade children who produced handwriting slowly and were also experiencing difficulty learning to write. In addition to the handwriting instruction provided in the classroom, all of the participating children received additional instruction from a specially trained instructor three times a week. The supplemental handwriting program was developed so that it addressed basic processes identified in several influential data-based models of handwriting performance (Ellis, 1982; Margolin, 1984;

van Galen, 1991). According to these models, writing a letter requires retrieving and holding the letter in working memory, accessing the corresponding motor program, setting the parameters for the program (e.g., establish the size of letter and speed of writing), and executing it. Correspondingly, students in the handwriting condition learned to name and identify the letters of the alphabet, were taught how to form each letter, adjusted parameters for speed or fluency by rewriting text at a faster pace, and practiced executing or writing letters in isolation, words, and sentences. These procedures were designed to teach students to write letters accurately and fluently.

Like the previous study by Berninger et al. (1997), students in the contact control condition received instruction in phonological awareness. This treatment was chosen because it is known to be beneficial to first-grade children (see Bus & van Ijzendoorn, 1999), and the data from the Berninger et al. (1997) study showed that teaching phonological awareness does not influence the process of learning to write letters.

◆ ◆ ◆

Discussion

Theoretical Implications

In this study, we examined if handwriting is a causal factor in learning to write. Previous research has shown that individual differences in handwriting skills are related to how much and how well children write (see Graham et al., 1997; Graham & Harris, 2000), and that early, supplementary handwriting instruction can boost the writing performance of poor handwriters immediately following instruction (Berninger et al., 1997; Jones & Christensen, 1999). To assess the causal role of handwriting in early writing development, we provided supplemental handwriting instruction to first grade children who were experiencing difficulty with handwriting and writing, and then assessed the immediate as well as long-term effects of such instruction.

> The findings from the current study indicate that handwriting is indeed causally related to learning to write.

The findings from the current study indicate that handwriting is indeed causally related to learning to write. Students who received supplementary handwriting instruction outperformed their counterparts in the contact control condition (i.e., phonological awareness instruction) on measures assessing not only handwriting, but writing skills as well. Immediately following instruction, students in the handwriting condition were more accurate in naming and writing the letters of the alphabet, and they were also able to produce the letters of

> **Most importantly, handwriting instruction resulted in immediate as well as more long-term improvements in students' compositional fluency skills.**

the alphabet and copy connected text more fluently. With the exception of copying text more fluently, these handwriting gains were maintained six months later. Most importantly, handwriting instruction resulted in immediate as well as more long-term improvements in students' compositional fluency skills. On a story writing probe, students in the handwriting condition composed at a much faster rate than their peers in the contact control condition at posttest (this measure was not administered at maintenance). Moreover, on a norm-referenced measure of compositional fluency, the Writing Fluency subtest from the WJ-R (Woodcock & Johnson, 1990), students in the handwriting condition were more skilled at constructing written sentences immediately after instruction and six months later. Consequently, the mastery of handwriting skills appears to facilitate not only the initial process of learning to write, as demonstrated by this and previous studies (Berninger et al., 1997; Jones & Christensen, 1999), but may also affect the outcomes of the learning process over time, at least up to a period of six months.

◆ ◆ ◆

Educational Implications

In recent years, there has been a tendency to downplay or even eliminate handwriting instruction as part of the writing program (Berninger, 1999; Graham & Weintraub, 1996), as approaches such as whole language and process writing have placed greater emphasis on content and process, and much less emphasis on form. The findings from the current study as well as the investigations by Berninger et al. (1997) and Jones and Christensen (1999), however, indicate that such an approach may be ill-advised with beginning writers who experience difficulty initially mastering the intricacies of handwriting. Students in these studies benefitted from explicit and supplemental instruction in how to form and fluently write the letters of the alphabet, as they evidenced improvements in both their handwriting and compositional skills. Thus, if educators want to improve the writing of these students, they need to focus not just on the content and process of writing, but on transcription skills such as handwriting as well.

It is also tempting to assume that the development of handwriting skills can be ignored because of the advent of alternative modes of composing, such as word processing and speech synthesis (Graham, 1992). As one teacher told the first author, "I don't need to worry much about handwriting, because everyone uses word processing today." Although the use of word processing and speech synthesis has clearly increased in recent years, beginning writers still, and for the foreseeable future, do most of their composing by hand. Unfortunately, the data from this study and clinical reports by others suggests that difficulties in developing adequate handwriting skills in the early grades may lead to arrested writing development, particularly in terms of compositional fluency. For example, third graders participating in a summer clinic at the University of Washington told investigators that they avoided writing, because their handwriting and spelling difficulties made it hard for others to read what they wrote (as reported in Berninger et al., 1997). Thus, until alternative methods of composing, such as word processing or speech synthesis, become the primary writing tool employed by beginning writers, handwriting should not be ignored in the early grades.

> ...students with an identified disability were just as likely to benefit from additional handwriting instruction as their non-disabled peers...

The outcomes from the current study as well as the two prior investigations (Berninger et al., 1997; Jones & Christensen, 1999) further indicate that supplemental handwriting instruction is an important element in preventing writing difficulties, at least for children who struggle to master handwriting skills in the early primary grades. The finding that students with an identified disability were just as likely to benefit from additional handwriting instruction as their nondisabled peers is particularly important because handwriting and writing difficulties are quite common among these students (Graham & MacArthur, 1987). The short-term intervention applied in this study shows that it may be possible to raise writing performance relative to same grade peers on a nationally normed test of compositional fluency. If compositional fluency can be raised by four-tenths of a standard deviation at posttest and six-tenths of a standard deviation six months later by 27, 15-minute sessions, it may be possible to raise performance even more by providing a longer intervention. Such improvements in compositional fluency may be especially important for struggling writers, as research by Berninger and her colleagues (Berninger et al., 1991) indicates that compositional fluency problems in the primary grades may be the genesis for writing problems in the upper grades.

Additional research is needed to replicate the current findings and to develop other techniques for preventing writing difficulties. A recent study by Berninger et al. (1998) indicates that early, supplemental spelling instruction may also be important in the prevention of writing difficulties. Extra spelling instruction improved both the spelling and compositional fluency of second grade students who were poor spellers. We further anticipate that early, supplemental instruction in the self-regulatory aspects of writing, particularly planning and revising, will help to prevent writing difficulties. Our own research has shown that struggling writers often experience difficulties regulating these processes when writing (De La Paz, Swanson, & Graham, 1998; Graham & Harris, 2000; Graham, 1997), and that directly teaching these processes to older elementary-level students who are poor writers results in improvements in how much and how well they write (Graham & Harris, 1996). It is also likely that efforts designed to increase the quantity and quality of the regular writing program will be beneficial as well. Such instruction should reduce the number of cases of writing failure due to poor instruction and help ameliorate the severity of writing difficulties experienced by other children whose primary problems are not instructional.

> ...explicit supplemental instruction that helps young children write letters accurately and quickly can increase the probability that they will become skilled writers.

In summary, explicit supplemental instruction that helps young children write letters accurately and quickly can increase the probability that they will become skilled writers. In the present study, such instruction was a better predictor of children's success than student or family variables or even the teachers' sense of efficacy or their approach to writing. This study, along with the investigations by Berninger et al. (1997) and Jones and Christensen (1999), shows that explicit handwriting instruction is an integral component of an effective writing program for beginning writers.

References

Berninger, V. (1999). Coordinating transcription and text generation in working memory during composing: Automatic and constructive processes. *Learning Disability Quarterly, 22,* 99-112.

Berninger, V., Mizokawa, D., & Bragg, R. (1991). Theory-based diagnosis and remediation of writing disabilities. *Journal of School Psychology, 29,* 57-97.

Berninger, V., Vaughn, K., Abbott, R., Abbott, S., Rogan, L., Brooks, A., Reed, E., & Graham, S. (1997). Treatment of handwriting problems in beginning writers: Transfer from handwriting to composition. *Journal of Educational Psychology, 89,* 652-666.

Berninger, V., Vaughn, K., Abbott, R., Brooks, A., Abbott, S., Rogan, L., Reed, E., & Graham, S. (1998). Early intervention for spelling problems: Teaching functional spelling units of varying size with a multiple-connections framework. *Journal of Educational Psychology, 90,* 587-605.

Briggs, D. (1980). A study of the influence of handwriting upon grades using examination scripts. *Educational Review, 32,* 185-193.

Bus, A., & van Ijzendoorn, M. (1999). Phonological awareness and early reading: A meta-analysis of experimental studies. *Journal of Educational Psychology, 91,* 403-414.

Chase, C. (1986). Essay test scoring: Interaction of relevant variables. *Journal of Educational Measurement, 23,* 33-41.

De La Paz, S., Swanson, P., & Graham, S. (1998). Contribution of executive control to the revising problems of students with writing and learning difficulties. *Journal of Educational Psychology, 90,* 448-460.

Ellis, A. (1982). Spelling and writing (and reading and speaking). In A. Ellis (Ed.), *Normality and pathology in cognitive functions* (pp. 113-146). London: Academic Press.

Graham, S. (1997). Executive control in the revising of students with learning and writing difficulties. *Journal of Educational Psychology, 89,* 223-234.

Graham, S. (1992). Issues in handwriting instruction. *Focus on Exceptional Children, 25,* 1-14.

Graham, S. (1990). The role of production factors in learning disabled students' compositions. *Journal of Educational Psychology, 82,* 781-791.

Graham, S., Berninger, V., Abbott, R., Abbott, S., & Whitaker, D. (1997). Role of mechanics in composing of elementary school students: A new methodological approach. *Journal of Educational Psychology, 89,* 170-182.

Graham, S., & Harris, K. (2000). The role of self-regulation and transcription skills in writing and writing development. *Educational Psychologist, 35,* 3-12.

Graham, S., & Harris, K.R. (1996). Self-regulation and strategy instruction for students with writing and learning difficulties. In S. Ransdell & M. Levy (Eds.), *Science of writing: Theories, methods, individual differences, and applications* (pp. 347-360). Mahwah, NJ: Erlbaum.

Graham, S., & MacArthur, C. (1987). Written language of the handicapped. In C. Reynolds & L. Mann (Eds.), *Encyclopedia of Special Education* (pp. 1678-1681). New York: Wiley & Sons.

Graham, S., & Weintraub, N. (1996). A review of handwriting research: Progress and prospects from 1980 to 1994. *Educational Psychology Review, 8,* 7-87.

Hughes, D.C., Keeling, B., & Tuck, B.F. (1983). Effects of achievement expectations and handwriting quality on scoring essays. *Journal of Educational Measurement, 20,* 65-70.

Jones, D., & Christensen, C. (1999). Relationship between automaticity in handwriting and students' ability to generate written text. *Journal of Educational Psychology, 91,* 44-49.

Margolin, D. (1984). The neuropsychology of writing and spelling: Semantic, phonological, motor, and perceptual processes. *The Quarterly Journal of Experimental Psychology, 36,* 459-489.

McCutchen, D. (1996). A capacity theory of writing: Working memory in composition. *Educational Psychology Review, 8,* 299-325.

Scardamalia, M., Bereiter, C., & Goleman, H. (1982). The role of production factors in writing ability. In M. Nystrand (Ed.), *What writers know: The language, process, and structure of written discourse* (pp. 173-210). New York: Academic Press.

van Galen, C. (1991). Handwriting: Issues for a psychomotor theory. *Human Movement Science, 10,* 165-191.

Woodcock, R., & Johnson, M. (1990). *Woodcock-Johnson Psycho-Educational Battery—Revised.* Chicago: Riverside.

How does handwriting support proficient writers?

Excerpts From

Relationship Between Automaticity in Handwriting and Students' Ability to Generate Written Text

Dian Jones and Carol A. Christensen:
University of Queensland

It appears that for children in the early years, orthographic-motor skills involved in handwriting have a significant effect on their ability to generate written text.

The ability to generate written text requires the execution of a complex array of cognitive and metacognitive skills. Because of the cognitive demands of this complexity, successful writers must be able to write letters and words automatically. This article reports 2 studies that examined the relationship between orthographic-motor integration related to handwriting and the ability to generate creative and well-structured written text. Participants in the first study were 114 Grade 1 students. When the effect of reading was controlled, orthographic-motor integration accounted for 67% of the variance in written expression. An intervention study with 19 students experiencing difficulty in handwriting and 19 students matched on gender and reading examined the impact of improving students' automaticity in handwriting. The intervention eliminated the detrimental effects on writing of lack of automaticity in orthographic-motor integration.

◆ ◆ ◆

Discussion

Although it was anticipated that there would be a significant relationship between orthographic-motor integration and the ability to express ideas in writing, the magnitude of the effect was surprising. In Grade 1, the correlation between handwriting and written expression was .73 when reading scores were partialed out. Thus, when reading was controlled, approximately 53% of the variance in story writing scores was accounted for by speed and accuracy in writing letters. Therefore, it appears that for children in the early years, orthographic-motor skills involved in handwriting have a significant effect on their ability to generate written text.

Although the studies reported here did not systematically investigate the range of areas that could be influenced by poor handwriting in the longer term, it seems a significant issue for future research to explore. If the impact of poor handwriting skills on written expression is largely consistent with these data, it could be hypothesized that persistent poor performance in written tasks will affect students' cognitive and affective development. This suggestion is similar to Stanovich's (1986) *Matthew effects* in reading. Stanovich argued that lack of automaticity in decoding skill resulted in negative experiences in early reading, which in turn led to avoidance of reading activities and further failure. Stanovich used the term *Matthew effects* because of the biblical reference to the "rich becoming richer." A similar cycle may exist in written expression for students who lack automaticity in handwriting. Failure in writing is likely to result in lower motivation to learn in the future, loss of self-efficacy, development of external locus of control, and avoidance of writing tasks (Ames, 1992; Bandura, 1986; Covington, 1983). Because of

> ...when reading was controlled, approximately 53% of the variance in story writing scores was accounted for by speed and accuracy in writing letters.

the relatively small amount of work that has been done in the area, the full costs of lack of automaticity in handwriting are not yet clearly understood.

Study 2 examined the impact of an intervention designed to enhance students' orthographic-motor integration skills. Nineteen students with handwriting difficulties were identified. To control for general language-related skills, these students were matched on reading with 19 classmates. At the beginning of the year, the control group had significantly better handwriting scores. Given the relationship between handwriting and written expression, it is not surprising that the control group was initially better at written expression than the intervention group.

After approximately 7 months of instruction, differences between the two groups had disappeared. This paints a very optimistic picture. It suggests that difficulty in handwriting is amenable to instruction. Further, it suggests that improvement in handwriting will result in comparable improvement in written expression.

Despite its efficacy, the intervention was not resource consuming. It was conducted in the regular classroom, planned by the class teacher following consultation with the researcher, and implemented by parent volunteers and teacher aides. This would seem to be a very cost-effective method of achieving what appear to be quite worthwhile gains in achievement.

It should be noted that the hypothesized relationship between orthographic-motor integration and written expression was seen to arise

> ...improvement in handwriting will result in comparable improvement in written expression.

from the multiple attentional demands of the task of generating written text. Lack of automaticity in writing resulted in students focusing on the orthographic-motor act of putting letters on the page rather than ideation, monitoring, and other cognitive aspects of text generation. The focus of the intervention, then, was to enhance children's automaticity in writing so that their letter formation became quick, smooth, and effortless. The goal of the intervention was not seen as producing "copybook" script.

It is unfortunate that in a number of cases, recent curricula reforms that have focused on meaningful learning have reduced the emphasis on practice activities that improve orthographic-motor skills related to handwriting. There may be unintended negative consequences for failing to ensure that all young children have sufficient practice in handwriting to be able to produce legible script at a level of automaticity.

References

Ames, C. (1992). Classrooms: Goals, structures and student motivation. *Elementary School Journal, 85,* 39-52.

Bandura, A. (1986). *Social foundations of thought and action: A social-cognitive theory.* Englewood Cliffs, NJ: Prentice Hall.

Covington, M.V. (1983). Motivated cognitions. In S.G. Paris, G.M. Olson, & H.W. Stevenson (Eds.), *Learning and motivation in the classroom* (pp. 139-164). Hillsdale, NJ: Erlbaum.

Stanovich, K. (1986). Matthew effects in reading: Some consequences of individual differences in the acquisition of literacy. *Reading Research Quarterly, 21,* 360-470.

Technology and the Oops! Effect: Finding a Bias Against Word Processing

M. D. Roblyer

In the four studies described here, raters have given word processed essays consistently lower grades than handwritten essays.

It has long been taken for granted that word processed essays receive higher scores than handwritten essays. But researchers have recently found that students actually get higher scores when they write their essays by hand. Read on to find out why this bias exists and how we can eliminate it.

Harvey Long—that icon of IBM instructional technology for nearly half a century—always used to get a laugh when he said "We shouldn't worry about computers taking over because we can always pull the plug. It's when the computer can turn around and put the plug back in that we'll be in trouble!" But Harvey never mentioned the time in which we now find ourselves: A time when we can't pull the plug on computers, even if we wanted to. Like the era after automobiles were introduced, when selecting a horse over a horseless carriage became increasingly illogical and, finally, impossible, the computer is a forced choice in more and more situations. And, as Edward Tenner points out in his recent book *Why Things Bite Back: New Technology and the Revenge Effect* (1996), some of the consequences of our "choice" to use technology are no laughing matter. Although there is no turning back on the path toward a largely computerized society, there are a number of negative effects that must be recognized and dealt with as best we can.

Tenner (1996) describes "revenge effects" as "ironic unintended consequences of mechanical, chemical, biological, and medical ingenuity" (p. 6). For example, introducing stronger football helmets to prevent head injuries has been found to increase the incidence of neck injuries in football, and use of computers to create the "paperless office" resulted in more paper being used instead of less.

This column explores research that indicates an effect of the kind that Tenner describes. Word processing, introduced into education to let teachers and students write easier, faster, and, therefore, better, can inadvertently discriminate against those who employ it. If we extract the hostile overtones in the word "revenge," we are left with what we might call "oops! effects," unanticipated negative outcomes that must be recognized and eliminated.

Documenting the Oops! Effect in Word Processing

Researchers seem to find consistent results when comparing ratings of handwritten and word processed papers. In the four studies described here, raters have given word processed essays consistently lower grades than handwritten essays.

Arnold, V., Legas, J., Obler, S., Pacheco, M., Russell, C., and Umbdenstock, L. (1990). *Do students get higher scores on their word processed papers? A study of bias in scoring handwritten versus word processed papers.* Whittier, CA: Rio Hondo College. (ERIC Document Reproduction No. ED 345 818)

Faculty at a Los Angeles-area college began this study because their experience had shown that raters consistently graded word processed papers higher than handwritten ones on a writing placement test. However, when they attempted to replicate this bias in a controlled study, they found the opposite. The same papers, when converted from handwritten to word processed format, received significantly lower ratings, and half the readers indicated a preference for reading handwritten papers. The researchers found that readers seemed to have higher expectations for word processed papers and were less likely to feel "closer to the writer" and "identify the writer's individual voice as a strong and important part of the essay" (p. 14). It also became apparent that printed text makes surface errors easier to see. One factor that may account for some of the difference between the previous findings and those in this study was the fact that students can choose between handwritten and word processed formats in the testing situation. Thus, those students who are already better writers may consistently have chosen to word process their essays for the writing placement test.

> The same papers, when converted from handwritten to word processed format, received significantly lower ratings....

Sweedler-Brown, C. (1992). Computers and assessment: The effect of typing versus handwriting on the holistic scoring of essays. *Journal of Research and Development in Education, 26*(I), 24–29.

Sweedler-Brown decided to do her study because past studies had found a consistent bias in favor of neatly handwritten papers over typed ones, a characteristic that she viewed as "one of the primary threats to the reliability and validity of holistic scoring" (p. 24). She wanted to see if training the raters to guard against "appearance bias" would diminish these effects. Each of 27 essays was transcribed in three graphic modes: word processed, nicely handwritten, and poorly handwritten. The same errors and text were present in each mode. Raters received special training to ensure that they would interpret and apply all scoring criteria accurately. Findings revealed significantly higher scores for neatly handwritten essays; no differences were found between typed and poorly handwritten ones. Regardless of rater training and essay quality, essays were much more likely to receive higher grades if they were neatly handwritten.

> **Regardless of rater training and essay quality, essays were much more likely to receive higher grades if they were neatly handwritten.**

Wolfe, E., Bolton, S., Feltovich, B., and Welch, C. (1993). *A comparison of word processed and handwritten essays from a standardized writing assessment.* Iowa City, IA: American College Testing Program. (ACT Research Report Series 93-8). (ERIC Document Reproduction No. ED 370 966)

Wolfe et al. focused on a high school writing program rather than a college program as previous studies had. Despite the enthusiasm for word processing exhibited by students who selected this format and their obvious use of printouts and spell-, grammar-, and style-checking features to help them revise essays, Wolfe et al. found results similar to those in previous studies, but even more dramatic. Scorers consistently gave transcribed papers lower ratings than original essays regardless of the original mode of composition. This was especially puzzling when a subsequent content analysis comparing handwritten and word processed originals showed that the word processed papers were longer and of substantially higher quality. The researchers observed that because students in this study selected their original mode of composition, the differences between essays may be attributable to student differences rather than differences in the mode of composition. A careful analysis of raters' scoring procedures revealed that raters used different processes to rate the two kinds of products. Also, they seemed to hold word processed papers to different and higher standards.

> Powers, D.E., Fowles, M., Farnum, M., and Ramsey, P. (1994). Will they think less of my handwritten essay if others word process theirs? Effects on essay scores of intermingling handwritten and word processed essays. *Journal of Educational Measurement, 31*(3), 220–233.

Like researchers in previous studies, Powers et al. converted essays to the opposite format and rescored them. Results again revealed higher average scores for handwritten essays. In trying to establish the source of this bias, Powers et al. found that word processed papers were perceived (incorrectly) to be shorter than handwritten ones. Although they adjusted for this perception by double-spacing the typed papers, the ratings for handwritten essays remained higher. But unlike Sweedler-Brown, Powers et al. found that training the raters did help decrease the bias. In a second study, Powers et al. trained new raters based on possible explanations for the bias and repeated the experiment. This time Powers et al. noticed a 25% reduction in the discrepancy. The effects in the second study were found to be so small that they were predicted to have little, if any, impact on decisions regarding placement and certification of students.

Why Does This Effect Occur and What Should We Do About It?

Word processing, like the automobile, is a technology that will not go away. Until word processing becomes the norm rather than an option, we must guard against the unanticipated outcomes we are seeing in writing assessments.

The reasons for raters' clear preference for handwritten essays over word processed ones seem to lie in the following three areas:

1. Raters seem to have higher expectations for typed essays.

2. Raters can spot text errors more easily in typed text.

3. Raters have more difficulty identifying the author's "voice" as an important part of the communication in typed text.

But knowing why the problem exists will only get us so far. How do we solve it? To begin, we need to make key personnel in writing programs aware of possible rater biases. These personnel often support word processing because they believe it will improve writing and that neatly typed papers will be easier for evaluators to read. They assume only positive effects, without considering a possible negative bias. If students have a choice between handwritten and word processed formats, no decisions should be made on placement or certification based on their writing tests until a negative bias has been screened for and eliminated.

Once key personnel are aware that a bias against word processed essays might exist, they should keep track of writing scores and determine if bias is present. They should also continue to monitor raters after antibias measures have been put into place to ensure that the problem has been resolved.

Finally, if a bias is found, raters should be trained to avoid it in a way that targets the specific source of the bias. Student training is also important. If students are required to word process their essays, they should be comfortable with the technology and have reliable, well-maintained equipment available throughout their writing program.

References

Tenner, E. (1996). *Why things bite back: New technology and the revenge effect*. London: Fourth Estate.

How does handwriting support proficient writers?

Chapter 6

A standard of legibility:
How should students' handwriting be evaluated?

"What do I get for just neatness?"

Reprinted by permission of Glenn Bernhardt.

Introduction

How should students' handwriting be evaluated? While it is easy to agree that student work should be legible, it can be difficult to arrive at an objective definition of *legibility* that teachers and students can use to evaluate handwriting. Is careless writing that can be deciphered with some effort *legible*? Should a student's writing closely conform to the models in a handwriting book in order to be called *legible*?

What is needed is a standard of legibility based on objective criteria that can be observed in students' writing. In general, legible writing is writing that can be easily read by a wide audience. While legible writing will exhibit personal style, it doesn't stray so far from the letter shapes on a standard alphabet chart that confusion occurs. This can be important advice for fifth or sixth graders who like to express themselves by adding curlicues to each letter or by writing in a small, cramped size. Legible writing is not "perfect penmanship," but it does show ease and consistency.

Zaner-Bloser emphasizes four "keys to legibility" that give criteria for legible handwriting in four areas—size, shape, slant, and spacing. The four keys form an assessment rubric that teachers and students can use to evaluate handwriting. Using the keys to legibility, students learn that legible handwriting is made up of letters with good shape and appropriate size, consistent slant, and regular spacing between letters, words, and sentences. More information about the four keys can be found in this chapter in "The Keys to Legibility," written by Zaner-Bloser author Clinton Hackney.

Once students learn to recognize legible handwriting, they should evaluate their writing regularly. When handwriting ceases to be evaluated, it tends to deteriorate. Unfortunately, this is what too often happens with older students and adults. To the extent that handwriting is evaluated regularly, it will continue to improve. The following types of evaluation should be included in every handwriting program.

Self-Evaluation

Students should use the keys to legibility to evaluate their own writing during handwriting instruction and in other subject areas. Developing the habit of thinking about legibility will help students whenever they write.

Teacher Evaluation

Teachers can emphasize handwriting by occasionally using a dual-marking system to give one mark for content-area work and another mark for handwriting. The Zaner-Bloser evaluation stamp, shown here, allows teachers and students to compare their evaluations based on the keys to legibility.

Zaner-Bloser Keys to Legibility Evaluation		
✓ if satisfactory	Student	Teacher
shape	O	O
straight up and down/slant	O	O
spacing	O	O
size	O	O

Peer Evaluation

Students can help each other by letting a partner know if his or her writing is clear and legible. This is an especially important step for writing partners who must read each other's rough drafts during the writing process.

Portfolio Assessment

Writing samples that show a student's handwriting progress can be included in a language arts portfolio or kept in a separate hand-writing folder. Samples should include handwriting practice as well as creative writing and work from other content areas. Challenge students to choose a weekly sample that represents their best handwriting to place in the portfolio.

The articles in this chapter provide important background information for teachers and administrators charged with setting a standard of legibility in their classrooms and schools. In "The Keys to Legibility," Clinton Hackney discusses four basic ways to evaluate handwriting. "Error Analysis in Handwriting" lists common hand-writing problems. "A Penchant for Penmanship" tells the story of one school that emphasizes handwriting, with amazing results. Finally, in "What Is Excellent Writing?" teacher Jim Henry shares his approach to portfolio assessment that includes a consideration of handwriting and spelling.

The Keys to Legibility

Clinton S. Hackney

The major criterion for evaluating student handwriting is legibility.

The goal of the teacher of handwriting is to develop in the student the skill of legible handwriting. If teachers are to be effective in teaching handwriting, they must find objective means of evaluating the student's progress toward that goal. Evaluation is needed to identify errors, and then to diagnose the cause of these difficulties.

Four Keys

It is important to determine those factors of legible handwriting that are to be evaluated. The keys to legible handwriting are: size, shape, slant, and spacing.

Size

Size refers to the relationship in height of the letters to each other and to the writing space. In the early elementary grades, writing is usually done on paper with wide rulings, as shown below. Tall letters touch the headline. Short letters touch the broken midline. A descender space is given for letters with descenders, such as y.

In later grades, students commonly use notebook paper for most of their writing. Beginning in grade 4 and above, the proportion of the letters does not change, but it is reduced to fit the smaller writing space, as shown below. Tall letters no longer touch the headline, and the writing paper does not have descender spaces.

good

Students can evaluate the size of their letters by drawing one horizontal line across the tops of all the tall letters and another across the tops of all the short letters in a writing sample, as shown below. Straight horizontal lines indicate that all letters are the correct size.

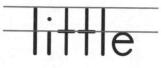

Shape

Shape describes the strokes that form each letter and give it a unique appearance. Using smooth, clear strokes ensures that each letter is distinct and easily recognized. When evaluating shape in their writing, students should examine the basic strokes that make up each letter. An alphabet chart of correct letter models displayed in the classroom will aid evaluation of shape.

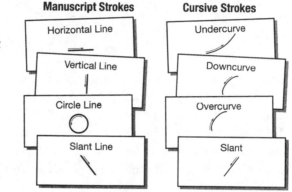

Slant

In manuscript writing, letters are vertical, so there should be no slant. The correct position of the paper and the proper direction in which the strokes are pulled prevents slant. Manuscript writing can be checked for consistent slant by drawing lines through the vertical strokes of the letters, as shown below.

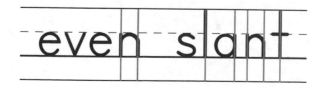

All cursive letters slant. The downstrokes or slant strokes of the letters should slant uniformly in the same direction. Cursive writing can be checked for consistent slant by drawing straight lines through the slant strokes of a writing sample, as shown below. If the lines are parallel, the slant is consistent; if they are at different angles, the slant is irregular.

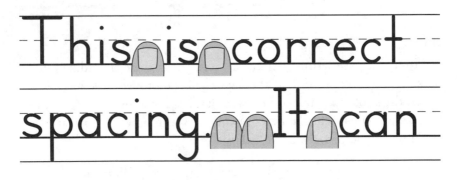

It is possible to have parallel strokes but still to have poor slant. Letters that are too vertical or too slanted result from tilting the paper either too much or too little. Remember that slant is determined by paper position, the direction in which the strokes are pulled, and the proper shifting of the paper.

Spacing

Spacing between letters, words, and sentences should be consistent. Achieving good spacing in manuscript writing can be difficult for young children. Evaluating spacing provides an excellent opportunity to train students in visual acuity. As the illustration below shows, this can be done by testing a writing sample to make sure there is enough space for one finger between words and two fingers between sentences. Letters should not touch each other, or be so far apart that confusion occurs.

How should students' handwriting be evaluated?

Because the letters are connected, good spacing is more easily achieved in cursive writing. Spacing can be evaluated by looking at a writing sample and making sure there is enough room for a small oval between letters, a slanted line between words, and an uppercase O between sentences, as shown below.

Using the Keys

The major criterion for evaluating student handwriting is legibility. Beginning writers do not have the muscle control to form letters using "perfect" strokes as well as they will when they are older. Thus, it makes sense to evaluate students' handwriting by comparing their work to writing samples done by students of the same age. This can be accomplished by taking a writing sample from students at least once in each grading period. Students can practice writing a sentence, and then write it again using their best handwriting.

Teachers should use the keys to legibility as criteria for comparing the samples and evaluating students' progress. The Zaner-Bloser Evaluation Guide for the appropriate grade level may be used. Evaluation Guides for grades one and three are shown below.

Grade I Evaluation Guide
Excellent—All keys acceptable

I like to write about playing with my friends.

Good—Three keys acceptable
(here, spacing is not acceptable)

I like to write
about playing with
my friends.

Average—Two keys acceptable
(here, slant and spacing are not acceptable)

I like to write
about play ing with
my friends.

Poor—No key acceptable

I like to write
about playing
with my friends.

Grade 3 Evaluation Guide
Excellent—All keys acceptable

This is a sample
of my best cursive
handwriting. How
am I doing?

How should students' handwriting be evaluated?

Good—Three keys acceptable
(here, slant is not acceptable)

This is a sample of my best cursive handwriting. How am I doing?

Average—Two keys acceptable
(here, slant and spacing are not acceptable)

This is a sample of my best cursive handwriting. How am I doing?

Poor—No key acceptable

This is a sample of my best cursive handwriting. How am I doing?

It is possible for a student to develop legible handwriting, pleasing in appearance and acceptable in all four keys to legibility, and yet not be able to transfer the skill to other subject areas where the emphasis is on content. The teacher may help the student transfer good handwriting to writing in the content areas by recognizing and valuing legibility in all written work. Spelling tests, math papers, and creative writing should all be occasionally evaluated for handwriting. When their handwriting is regularly evaluated, students will begin to make a habit of remembering "the four s's"—size, shape, slant, and spacing—whenever they write.

Error Analysis in Handwriting

C. Glennon Rowell

The easiest letters to make, as expected, had the fewest errors.

Factors other than letter formation leading to illegibility in handwriting include such errors as retracing, lack of alignment, and incorrect size of letters. One study which continues to be repeated in current literature, was conducted by Lewis and Lewis and dealt with first-graders' performance in manuscript. (Lewis & Lewis, 1965)... Specific errors found in the Lewis and Lewis study included:

1. The letters **N, d, q,** and y were the most frequently reversed letters.

2. The letter **m** had the greatest number of partial omissions, followed by **U** and **I**.

3. Incorrect size was the most frequent type of error. Although more evenly distributed among the letters than any other type of error, it was more prevalent among the descending letters, **p, g, y, q,** and **j**.

4. Letters most frequently misshaped were **j, G,** and **J**.

5. Incorrect relationship of parts of letters was a common error and occurred most frequently in **k, R, a, M,** and **m** in decreasing order of frequency.

6. Incorrect placement relative to line was a common error in the descending letters but less frequent in other letters.

7. Additions were more frequent in letters **q, C, k, m,** and **Y**.

8. Errors were more common where curves and vertical lines merge (**J, U, f, h, j, m, n, r,** and **u**).

9. Boys were more prone to error than were girls. (Lewis & Lewis, 1965)

The easiest letters to make, as expected, had the fewest errors. These were **l, o, L, O,** and **H**. (Lewis & Lewis, 1965) These letters are easy to make because they are composed of the simplest strokes, (vertical and horizontal lines), and the **o** requires no merging of different kinds of strokes.

In a study that was more recent than the Lewis and Lewis study, R. Stennett, P. Smithe, and M. Hardy report that their K-3 subjects had

How should students' handwriting be evaluated?

more trouble copying lowercase manuscript letters than uppercase letters. The most difficult letters for the subjects in this study were r, u, h, and t which have been identified as letters requiring more visuomotor control. The easiest letters to make were o, l, s, and c, all letters made with a single stroke. (Peck et al., 1983)

The Horton study on illegibilities of sixth graders' writing is one of the most recent studies in which errors in cursive writing were identified. Over 1000 specimens of writing were collected. As reported earlier, h, i, k, p, z, and r accounted for 30% of all errors made. (Froese) While Horton primarily concentrated on error malformations (of lowercase letters only), some information was provided about left-handed versus right-handed boys and girls. This information, plus some additional information on errors made in general, follow:

1. Errors on forming letters a, b, c, i, l, m, n, u, v, and x accounted for only 12 percent of the total errors made by the group studied (compared to r which alone accounted for 12 percent of the errors made).

2. Left-handed boys made a higher percentage of illegibilities than did any other group, with letters d, e, h, z, g, n, q, and r presenting the most trouble for these students.

3. Left-handed girls had more trouble with r, o, h, and q than with other letters.

4. Right-handed boys had the most difficulty with formation of letters r and g, with malformations of these two letters accounting for 25 percent of these pupils' problems.

5. Right-handed girls had more trouble with r, h, and z than with other letters. Problems with these three letters accounted for 37 percent of the problems of this group. (Horton, 1970)

References

Froese, Victor. Handwriting: practice, pragmatism, and progress, in *Research in the Language Arts—Language and Schooling*, eds. Victor Froese and Stanley B. Straw (Baltimore: University Park Press, 1981), p. 236.

Horton, Lowell W. (1970). Illegibilities in the cursive handwriting of sixth-graders. *The Elementary School Journal, 70:* 446-50.

Lewis, Edward R. and Hilda P. Lewis (1965). An analysis of errors in the formation of manuscript letters by first-grade children. *American Educational Research Journal, 2:* 27-34, 37.

Peck, Michaeleen, Eunice N. Askov, and Steven H. Fairchild (1983). Another decade of research in handwriting. *Journal of Educational Research, 73:* 284.

Handwriting Research and Resources. A Guide to Curriculum Planning

141

A Penchant for Penmanship

From *Learning*

Teachers at Blackshear Elementary are
big believers in the power of the pen.

———————————

Blackshear Elementary was a school in trouble. Teachers were complaining that students weren't up to grade level, parents were frustrated, and principal George Mundine knew that he needed to make some changes—and fast. What the school needed was a common goal to serve as an anchor, Mundine thought, a goal that everyone would value and agree on. But what kind of goal would work for this inner-city Houston school, whose students by and large were poor and whose parents' support would be hard to win? Then it came to him—they would concentrate on handwriting.

That was more than 20 years ago. Since then, Blackshear has been recognized as one of the best elementary schools in the country, and its reputation as "the handwriting school" has grown locally and nationally. The focus on handwriting serves as a springboard for student achievement across the curriculum and remains the school's focus today.

What's the Big Deal?

Some people might see handwriting as an old-fashioned skill and wonder why Blackshear chose it as its focus. One reason is that it's a skill many students can experience success with, especially kids who might not find much success in science fairs or on standardized tests. "Handwriting isn't an academic, book kind of thing," says Estella Ford, school counselor at Blackshear. "It's a motor skill students can learn."

Another reason for focusing on handwriting is that it helps students develop pride in their work and helps build their self-esteem, says first-grade teacher Jacqueline Adams. "Children can feel good that they have already mastered one life skill," she says—especially a skill that they see reflected in the world around them.

Good handwriting can also help a student convey a positive impression to the outside world, Mundine says. "When you walk into a room, how you look and how you present yourself tell a lot about you," he tells the students. "Handwriting is the same way. When you put that pen to

How should students' handwriting be evaluated?

paper, your penmanship is the first thing that a person sees, and it tells a lot about you."

Real-World Concerns

Business leaders nationwide are likely to applaud Blackshear's focus on this life skill. According to research in *American Demographics* magazine, illegible handwriting costs American business $200 million annually. According to the same research, 90 percent of business executives complain of poor handwriting among employees, and 40 percent say that handwriting is getting worse. The U.S. postal service spends $4 million annually to decipher and deliver 38 million illegibly addressed letters. Handwriting legibility plays a role in safety, too. In a survey of pharmacists conducted by Zaner-Bloser and Parker Pen, 85 percent say that illegible handwriting causes errors or safety hazards.

Parents are strong supporters of Blackshear's focus on handwriting. When they visit the school, one of the first things they see is a display of handwriting samples—one from every student. "That's very meaningful to parents,"

> **The focus on handwriting serves as a springboard for student achievement across the curriculum and remains the school's focus today.**

Ford says. "Too often when they come to school, they see only the very best work displayed." Fifth-grade teacher Howard Bonner adds, "There's evidence of good penmanship all over Blackshear, from the hallways to the classrooms to the foyer."

People outside the school are quick to notice and praise the students' handwriting skills. Both second-grade teacher Nina Suan and sixth-grade teacher Edna Davis have had children in their classes win creative-writing contests. In each case, the judges reported being impressed not only with the children's creativity but also with the neatness and beauty of their handwriting.

A Star Is Born

Here's how the handwriting program works at Blackshear: Every class turns in a set of handwriting samples to Mundine each Friday. Then on Monday, each grade's Handwriting Star of the Week is announced on the school's radio station. "Students are so proud when their names are called out as Handwriting Stars," Suan says. "Their faces glow. They want to get that reward and recognition."

Being named the Handwriting Star can be a turning point for some students, Adams says. When Derrick came to her class, for example, he was withdrawn and never smiled. "I tried everything with him," she says. "I praised him and gave him special rewards. I made him group leader of his table." Although she made a little progress, she knew she still hadn't cracked Derrick's shell. "The day I told Derrick that his handwriting was going to be on the front of the samples that I was turning in to our principal was the day the light came on in his eyes," she says. "He gave me a hug and a smile." And when Derrick's name was announced as the first-grade Handwriting Star of the Week, he grinned from ear to ear.

Us, Too?

Blackshear's emphasis on handwriting extends beyond the students—teachers are also expected to practice good penmanship. When Title I coordinator Shirley McConico first joined the faculty as a regular classroom teacher, her weekly lesson plans were returned from the principal with a note about the quality of her own penmanship. "After that, I took a teacher's manual, and while I taught the students how to use correct penmanship, I also had to teach myself," McConico says. "I finally realized the importance of handwriting and the impact it has on my students." Since then, McConico has presented workshops all over her school district on using handwriting as a tool for teaching reading.

Outstanding handwriting can be found even in the principal's office—Mundine has a reputation for having excellent penmanship. Has it helped him get where he is today? "I imagine so," he says. "It certainly hasn't hurt."

How should students' handwriting be evaluated?

What Is Excellent Writing?

Jim Henry

**My students needed to develop an awareness
of the characteristics of effective writing.**

I moved toward portfolio assessment in my first-grade classroom when I realized that the kind of learning that was taking place could not be measured by unit tests and worksheets. My students were involved in problem solving. They were developing an understanding that there were often many ways to get to an answer and often many correct answers to a problem. In language arts, my students were choosing their own writing projects to work on and sharing their work with others. I valued this learning greatly, and I sought a form of assessment that could capture some of this magic. Portfolio assessment seemed the perfect solution.

Initially, I was thrilled with our portfolio system; my students' individual accordion folders bulged with projects. I panicked in February, however, when, while preparing students for a second round of portfolio sharing with their parents, I discovered that their writing wasn't improving. There was more of it, but there was little change in quality.

My students needed to develop an awareness of the characteristics of effective writing. I knew that I couldn't just dump a list of writing characteristics on them. To be meaningful, the writing criteria had to come from them.

Modeling Self-Assessment

I keep my own portfolio of many of the projects that I created with the kids during writing sessions. I've saved poems, songs, letters, nonfiction, and fiction, including our rendition of stories with highly predictable texts.

Sitting before my class, I emptied out my portfolio for all to see. I hadn't looked at the selections for a while, and I referred to them in a manner similar to how one might recollect old friends. I told the kids how I loved all these projects, and that they were all good. But, I told them, even though they were all good, some were a little more special to me than others. Then I labeled three index cards: *Good, Very Good,* and *Excellent.* We discussed the words, then I decorated each card with crayons and taped them to the chalkboard to serve as headings.

I then reviewed each project and placed them under one of the headings. Students heard me thinking the process aloud (I tried not to divulge formal criteria for my decisions—we'd get to that later) and soon wanted to make decisions for me, but I told them that these decisions were mine. I wanted them to understand that a portfolio is a self-assessment tool, and that the decisions involved belong to its owner.

Students Self-Assess

I gave a set of the three labeled index cards—which I prepared ahead of time—to each student to decorate. Soon the class was happily decorating the headings. I invited them to evaluate their portfolio projects, and students began poring over their portfolios, asking one another for advice. The conversations were rich with comparisons. I walked around the room and asked questions about their decisions.

Kneeling beside Todd's desk, I glanced at his journal entry about a family trip to the zoo. It was filled with sentence fragments and missing capital letters. I asked him why he had placed this under the *excellent* heading. With a huge grin he answered that his visit to the zoo was one of the greatest days of his life. I realized then that the criteria we would develop as a class would have to reflect far more than my mechanics-oriented goals.

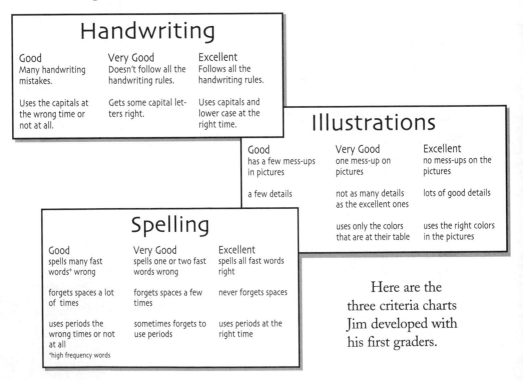

Handwriting

Good	Very Good	Excellent
Many handwriting mistakes.	Doesn't follow all the handwriting rules.	Follows all the handwriting rules.
Uses the capitals at the wrong time or not at all.	Gets some capital letters right.	Uses capitals and lower case at the right time.

Illustrations

Good	Very Good	Excellent
has a few mess-ups in pictures	one mess-up on pictures	no mess-ups on the pictures
a few details	not as many details as the excellent ones	lots of good details
	uses only the colors that are at their table	uses the right colors in the pictures

Spelling

Good	Very Good	Excellent
spells many fast words* wrong	spells one or two fast words wrong	spells all fast words right
forgets spaces a lot of times	forgets spaces a few times	never forgets spaces
uses periods the wrong times or not at all	sometimes forgets to use periods	uses periods at the right time
*high frequency words		

Here are the three criteria charts Jim developed with his first graders.

How should students' handwriting be evaluated?

Developing a Class Chart

After everyone had sorted their work into three piles, I wrote the three headings at the top of a sheet of chart paper. "What's the difference between an excellent project and a good one?" I asked. "What would you need to do to change a very good project into an excellent one?"

The children began to look at their portfolio selections with a more critical eye. "My excellent projects have color in their drawing," one student offered. "My handwriting is better in these," said another. "[My excellent pieces] are longer. I spent more time working on them," said a third child. With each student's comment, children glanced back at their work and reevaluated their decisions based on the unfolding criteria of their peers. However, I began to sense that students were devaluing projects that they hadn't deemed excellent. I reaffirmed the worth of the "nonexcellent" efforts by pointing out that many of these projects were rough drafts.

We continued to make observations about the characteristics of effective writing, recording our ideas on the chart paper. We made inferences: If an excellent project had all correct spelling, what might a very good project have? And how many misspelled words could a good project have? We agreed that an excellent project should have no spelling mistakes. My first graders raised their hands, eager to contribute to the discussion. I knew then that their writing would never be the same.

Adding to the Chart

For the rest of the year, our chart grew as students refined their ideas about effective writing. The students went about adding to the chart in a grassroots, democratic way that went beyond my expectation. For example, at one point during an informal portfolio conference with me, a student commented that all of her excellent projects had illustrations that used more than one color. She then recommended to the class that this characteristic be added to the chart. Another student picked up a copy of *Blueberries for Sal* by Robert McCloskey and said that this was an excellent book and that it had only one color. After discussion, the students decided that not every excellent project had to have every excellent characteristic from the chart.

Long-Term Benefits

The writing criteria my students hammered out thoroughly infused their work and their thinking. During class portfolio sharing, students often referred to the project they were presenting as excellent or very good, and articulated their reasons for thinking this. And I often observed students evaluating their projects with their three cards laid out on their desk. To ensure that the writing criteria stayed fresh in their minds, we formally did the index card activity each quarter.

I still have questions about the proper role of portfolio assessment in a first-grade classroom. Nonetheless, this process has provided my students and me with an opportunity to develop writing criteria.

Chapter 7

How can we meet students' individual needs in handwriting?

THE GRAPHOLOGIST AT WORK

Spiky letters... doesn't understand human nature. Small vowels...unimaginative

Should remain a physician, and give up foolish plan to become a writer.

Downward slant... timidity. Capitals... withdrawn, unaggressive. Should learn to be assertive.

Closed 'C'... desire to stay close to home. Wavy underline... fear of water. Would be happiest as a shepherd.

© 1994 by Sidney Harris— *The Chronicle of Higher Education*

Introduction

How can we meet students' individual needs in handwriting? Children can experience difficulties with handwriting for a number of reasons. The most common reason is that too little class time has been devoted to handwriting instruction and practice. Before concluding that a student has a special need in the area of handwriting, it is important for teachers to make sure that ample time has been given to master the skill.

But what about the student who exhibits consistent, long-term problems with handwriting? Slow, labored writing; misshapen letters; difficulty sequencing and arranging words on paper; an inability to write for a sustained period of time—all of these signs can point to a more serious problem. Sometimes, conditions such as attention deficit disorder, dyslexia, dysgraphia, and poor motor control can prevent a student's success in handwriting.

Many students with special needs receive individualized instruction outside of the classroom. However, teachers can aid progress in handwriting for these students by analyzing their needs and providing clear, consistent instruction. One of the best ways to do this is by determining whether students learn best when information is presented in a *visual* mode, an *auditory* mode, or a *kinesthetic* mode.

Activities that benefit the kinesthetic learner involve touch and movement. Walking on giant letters taped on the floor, tracing sandpaper letters, and writing in the air are all good activities for the kinesthetic learner. Kinesthetic activities are also appropriate for students with attention deficit disorder. Auditory learners need opportunities to listen and verbalize. Instructions should be given in clear, consistent language. Listening to stroke descriptions on an audiotape and verbalizing the strokes used to make letters are good exercises for auditory learners. Visual learners need good letter models with directional arrows. Before writing a letter, these students should be encouraged to look at it as a whole, noting its unique shape and attributes.

In addition, teachers can use the following suggestions to design lessons that address students' special needs in handwriting.

Offer help with directionality and letter reversals.

Make arrows on students' papers to help them remember to write from left to right, and color the left edge green to show where to begin. For students who reverse letters, emphasize the individual strokes in each letter and encourage students to say the stroke names as they write.

Provide materials that support students.

Don't be afraid to use paper with wide rulings for students who are having trouble. Increase the size of the pencil for students who "squeeze" the writing instrument. Show the alternate method of holding the pencil between the first and second fingers, as shown below. Allow students to use this pencil grip if it feels more comfortable.

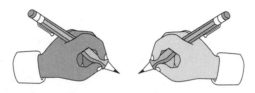

Give short, frequent lessons in handwriting basics.

If possible, teach a handwriting lesson daily for no more than 15 minutes. Emphasize the basic strokes that make up each letter of the alphabet. Encourage students with poor sustained muscle control to lift their pencil frequently when they write manuscript letters if the continuous-stroke approach is difficult for them.

Emphasize legibility, not perfection.

Provide opportunities for older students to use manuscript writing, if it is easier for them. Surround students with models of acceptable handwriting and set a good example when you write on the chalkboard and on students' papers.

The articles in this chapter provide a full spectrum of practical suggestions for the teacher of students with special needs in handwriting. The characteristics of dyslexia and dysgraphia are discussed in "Handwriting: What It Can Tell You About Your Students." Lisa Kurtz presents solutions to common handwriting problems in "Helpful Handwriting Hints." In "Helping Hands: A World of Manipulatives to Boost Handwriting Skills," June Naus details ways to support handwriting success in all areas of the early childhood curriculum. Finally, "Teaching the Left-Handed Writer" explains how teachers can help an often-overlooked population.

Handwriting: What It Can Tell You About Your Students

From *Learning*

...misformed letters...can be clues that the child is headed
for bigger problems down the road.

When kindergarten students print their names using letters like the ones shown below, you might figure, "Katie's just learning to print. She'll get the hang of it," or "Jason's printing is sloppy. He needs to take his time." But misformed letters like these can be clues that the child is headed for bigger problems down the road.

Children who make an excessive number of these types of printing errors, called *form errors,* are at an increased risk for failure in first and second grades, according to Marvin L. Simner, Ph.D., a researcher and professor at the University of Western Ontario in London, Ontario. In fact, in one study Dr. Simner found that 78 percent of the kindergartners who were rated by their teachers as making an excessive number of these form errors later received D's on their first-grade report cards.

Typical form errors

How can we meet students' individual needs in handwriting?

What's the Reason?

Parents and teachers are quick to assume that kids who make these kinds of errors have a problem with visual perception or fine motor skills. But Dr. Simner's research shows that's not usually the case. Instead, these children seem to have trouble remembering the shapes of the letters or planning the sequence of strokes needed to form the letters, leading to a B with too many bumps or an S with extra curves.

While giving the students extra help with handwriting may cure a symptom, it doesn't address an underlying problem, Dr. Simner says. Teachers should watch the children's overall language development and progress across the curriculum. Unless these children get extra help in reading and language, as well as in handwriting, they may slip through the cracks.

Two Common Problems

Another quick assumption that both parents and teachers sometimes make is that if a student reverses letters, he has dyslexia. Dyslexia is only one type of learning disability that can manifest itself through handwriting. Another prevalent condition is called dysgraphia. Both are problems that children can often overcome, with appropriate help.

Dyslexia

According to estimates from the National Institutes of Health, as many as 15 percent of your students may have dyslexia. Dyslexia is a problem rooted in language development, not vision—dyslexics don't see words and letters backward. Reversing and transposing letters aren't good indicators of whether a child is dyslexic. Instead, watch for:

- difficulty understanding the connection between individual letters and the sounds they make in combination or how syllables fit together
- difficulty decoding words
- difficulty with spelling
- a tendency to get numbers or letters out of order when reading or writing them
- poor reading comprehension
- incorrect or incomplete understanding of what the student hears
- difficulty expressing thoughts in writing
- confusion with left and right

- difficulty with the sequence of steps in math problems or doing math problems in the wrong direction—adding or subtracting from right to left instead of left to right, for example
- other family members with similar problems

Diagnosing and treating dyslexia early seem to be the keys to helping students overcome the problem. One study of 10,000 students showed that when dyslexic kids were identified in first or second grade, 82 percent were back on grade level in two years. When help was delayed until third grade, only 47 percent were back on grade level in two years. And only 8 percent of kids identified in sixth grade were on grade level in the same time frame.

Dysgraphia

A condition that overlaps with dyslexia is dysgraphia, which has been characterized as "a missing link in the ability to transfer what's in the mind to the pencil point." In other words, students understand what they hear and read, but the actual act of writing is difficult for them. Children with dysgraphia may not be able to write legibly. As many as ten percent of your students could have dysgraphia, with boys and left-handed students more likely to be affected. Watch for:

- poor penmanship
- writing that runs off the page
- poor spelling
- verbal skills that are significantly better than the student's writing skills
- difficulty remembering the shapes of letters
- holding a pencil or pen with a tight grip
- poor wrist, body, and paper position
- excessive erasing
- mixing uppercase and lowercase or printed and cursive letters

How to Help

Mark Westervelt, a language tutor and handwriting consultant at the Jemicy School, a school for dyslexic and dysgraphic students in Owings Mills, Md., says that dyslexic and dysgraphic students typically need additional direct instruction to help them overcome their

How can we meet students' individual needs in handwriting?

problems. He offers several suggestions that you can use to help all of your students, regardless of whether they have a learning disability.

Compare handwriting with baseball.

Get a bat and demonstrate a poor batting stance in front of your students. Have them explain to you why you won't be able to hit the ball correctly if your hands are in the wrong position. Explain that the same principles apply to how the kids sit and how they hold a pencil when writing. Then help them improve and practice their "handwriting stance" by becoming a handwriting coach.

Watch how students form their letters.

Some letters may look fine, but the student may make the strokes in the wrong order, causing her to write slowly. As the rest of the class picks up speed, she'll fall behind.

Check to see if kids are developing muscle memory—the process of ingraining the actual act of writing a letter into the muscles.

One quick way to do this is to ask students to close their eyes and write the letters of the alphabet in order in groups of three. Students who can write "automatically" have developed muscle memory.

The State of the Art

Handwriting is a very personal mode of expression that researchers are working to better understand. Test your handwriting knowledge by reviewing these popular myths and facts.

STATEMENT	MYTH OR FACT?
Struggles with handwriting affect between 12 percent and 21 percent of students.	**Fact.** Estimates run as high as 44 percent for students in urban areas.
Teachers aren't spending time teaching handwriting anymore.	**Myth.** Teachers in grades K–6 spend an average of 30 to 60 minutes per week teaching handwriting, according to a recent national survey.
After third grade, students no longer need handwriting instruction.	**Myth.** A study in the Netherlands showed that when formal handwriting instruction stopped after third grade, students' handwriting became less legible.

STATEMENT	MYTH OR FACT?
Girls are better at handwriting than boys are.	**Fact.** Girls' handwriting tends to have more clearly formed letters and better overall quality. Girls also tend to write faster than boys.
Right-handed people's writing is easier to read than left-handed people's.	**Myth.** The latest research shows no difference in quality or legibility.
The better the child's handwriting, the higher the child's I.Q.	**Myth.** Studies have found no consistent correlations between handwriting and I.Q.
Good visual perception skills are crucial for good handwriting.	**Myth.** Of course good visual skills help. But surprisingly, these skills aren't crucial. When researchers compared the handwriting quality of groups of first and sixth graders with their scores on visual perception tests, they didn't find a significant link.
In cursive writing, a few letters tend to be the ones that are most often written illegibly.	**Fact.** Four letters—**a, e, r,** and **t** account for almost half of the misformed, hard-to-decipher letters at any grade.
Insisting that students stick to one handwriting model helps them become better at handwriting.	**Myth.** Students inevitably develop a personal handwriting style, so insisting that they stick to a particular model only frustrates them—and you, too.
Teaching kids to "talk through" how to form a letter helps them get it right.	**Fact.** This approach does help some students, but most make only modest gains. Talking through letters is a temporary aid that students should abandon as soon as they're ready.
Students who print poorly become poor cursive writers, too.	**Myth.** Researchers collected printing samples from 137 third graders just prior to their learning cursive. Later they collected samples of the students' cursive writing. They found only small to moderate links between the quality of the printing and the quality of the cursive writing.
Most students with handwriting problems have dyslexia.	**Myth.** Some students, in fact, are dyslexic. But many more simply are immature or haven't been taught proper handwriting skills.

How can we meet students' individual needs in handwriting?

Helpful Handwriting Hints

Lisa A. Kurtz

This article presents practical solutions to some of the more common problems that may interfere with the mechanics of writing.

Classroom teachers should consider handwriting instruction to be a relevant part of the elementary-level curriculum because of the role written communication plays in a total literacy program. While the content of a student's written effort is admittedly more important than its appearance, some degree of proficiency in the mechanical aspects of writing is needed to prevent interruption in the flow of communicative intent. Teachers should consider remedial instruction not only when the student's writing is illegible, but also whenever the student writes so slowly or with such effort that it interferes with concentration on the content of the assignment. They can do much to reinforce remedial handwriting strategies for children with motor learning difficulties. This article presents practical solutions to some of the more common problems that may interfere with the mechanics of writing.

Poor Sitting Posture

Poor posture often relates to an underlying problem with low muscle tone and can significantly interfere with the ease with which a child can coordinate hand movement for visually guided work. The child should have a chair that has a flat seat and back. The chair should be at a height that allows the child's feet to rest flat with the hips, knees, and ankles all at 90-degree angles. This will help the child to achieve smooth postural adjustments as the writing arm moves across the paper. The desk height should be 2 inches above the height of the child's bent elbows (Benbow, 1988). If the desk is too high, the child will tend to elevate his or her shoulders, which can restrict freedom of movement. If the desk is too low, the child may tend to slouch over the desk or lean on the nondominant arm for support. When copying material from the chalkboard, children with writing difficulties should be seated directly in front of the material to be copied, because fine motor skill tends to be most efficient when the child is in a symmetrical body position.

Immature Pencil Grasp

Children who persist in using primitive pencil grasps may demonstrate problems with low muscle tone and may have failed to develop the ability to isolate distal movements. Their control of hand movements comes from the shoulder and elbow, as opposed to the more precise control that comes from the hand and fingers. While some degree of individual variability is acceptable, it is important to reinforce the following elements of pencil grasp (Benbow, 1988):

1. The forearm should rest on the writing surface in a neutral position, with the hand resting on the little finger. This position allows the wrist to move freely.

2. The wrist should be in a slightly extended posture (bent back), because this brings the thumb in a position where it can comfortably oppose the fingers.

3. There should be a rounded, open web space between the thumb and fingers. This position permits freedom of movement through all finger joints and also allows the finger pads to contact the pencil shaft. Tactile sensors are most efficient on the pads of the fingers, so this position optimizes sensory awareness of grip pressure and kinesthetic movements. One of the best activities for encouraging proper hand position is to practice writing, tracing, or other fine motor activities while sitting or standing at a vertical work surface, such as a blackboard or easel. When the work is presented at or slightly below eye level, the student cannot avoid holding the writing tool using the desired wrist position.

> One of the best activities for encouraging proper hand position is to practice...while sitting or standing at a vertical work surface, such as a blackboard or easel.

Children who persist in using primitive types of pencil grasps may benefit from a variety of sensorimotor activities and exercises. Games that provide deep pressure to the shoulder joints, such as wheelbarrow walking or crawling on hands and knees through an obstacle course, may be appropriate in helping such children increase control and stability at the shoulder (Oliver, 1989). Some children enjoy learning the sign language alphabet as a fun way to practice finger isolation skills. Children with weak pencil grasps may benefit from resistive pencil activities such as tracing around stencils or templates, drawing or writing in clay with a stylus, or drawing on sandpaper or pressure-sensitive carbons. The resistance causes the child to grip the writing tool more firmly, to receive increased sensory feedback and subsequently to strengthen hand muscles.

Adapted pencil holders such as triangle grips or Stetro grips may be useful for children who have difficulty remembering the proper position but have adequate control when the pencil is placed for them. Teachers can also adapt standard pencils by wrapping them with strips of tape or adhesive-backed foam padding to mark where on the shaft the pencil should be held. Old-fashioned pencil holders that keep the pencil in a vertical position are also helpful for some children, because they encourage approach and grasp with the forearm in the proper position.

Poor Stability or Positioning of Paper

Several associated characteristics may be evident in children who have trouble positioning or stabilizing the paper. These include the following:

1. There may be a tendency to switch hands frequently during manipulative play. This suggests that the child is not certain of which hand to assign a dominant role and which hand to use as an assistor.

2. Synkinesis, or motor overflow, may be observed in the less dominant hand. For example, when performing a one-handed activity, the other hand moves involuntarily.

3. There may be hesitancy or discomfort in manually or visually crossing the midline of the body. This is often a subtle problem that may be present only as a stiffness in trunk movements when writing. For example, when writing at the chalkboard the child may step sideways rather than allowing the writing arm to reach past the midline.

To help children who have difficulties with bilateral motor integration, teachers should encourage activities that require the two hands to work reciprocally. The easiest bilateral activities require using the two hands symmetrically, as in clapping games or flattening clay with a rolling pin. Slightly more difficult activities allow the nondominant hand to be in a static role while the dominant hand assumes a more dynamic role. Examples include holding a mixing bowl while stirring with the dominant hand and holding a template steady while the dominant hand traces. The most challenging bilateral activities require both hands to interact reciprocally and with different motions. Scissor activities offer this sort of experience, because one hand manipulates the scissors while the other holds and orients the angle of the paper.

Adjusting the angle of the paper may help some children with poor bilateral coordination. While good writers seem to learn best using a slight slant, increasing the slant of the paper and shifting it slightly toward the dominant hand may help a child who avoids crossing the midline, because it places the paper to the side of the midline. Once the best angle has been identified for the student, a strip of masking tape can serve as a visual reference. When a child has severe difficulty stabilizing the paper during writing, a blotter or large sheet of construction paper taped to the desk may provide just enough friction to keep the paper from slipping.

Uncertain Hand Dominance

If a student has not clearly demonstrated a preferred hand by 1st grade, the decision should be made for the student based on observations of which hand is better coordinated. If teachers and parents feel unclear about which is the more skilled hand, it is probably wise to request consultation from an occupational therapist or other motor skills specialist before encouraging the use of either hand. Once a preferred hand is identified, teachers may reinforce the student's awareness by placing jewelry or a ribbon on that wrist.

Children with delayed hand dominance or hesitancy in crossing the midline of the body will tend to reach for objects with whichever hand happens to be the closest. Most school-aged children will retain the object in the grasping hand, even if its use requires reaching across the midline. For this reason, the student's work area should be organized so that materials are located on the same side of the desk as the preferred hand.

Difficulty Copying from the Chalkboard

Problems in this area can result from a variety of factors, including poor short-term visual memory, poor visual perception (especially figure-ground separation), or poor eye-muscle control. Students with this type of difficulty should be seated as close to the chalkboard as possible.

They may benefit from having the teacher write only small amounts on the chalkboard at any one time or use different colored chalk to write different portions of the material. When older students are required to copy large amounts of material from the chalkboard, teachers may consider offering them a copy of the teacher's plan to copy from near point.

Problems with Spatial Organization

For students who have difficulty with spacing, prompts such as placing a finger between words may serve as a helpful reminder. If the student has trouble remembering to write from left to right, the teacher may run a length of green tape for *Go* along the left side of the desk, and red tape for *Stop* along the right side. For the student who forgets to leave left or right margins on the page, a clear strip of tape run along the side of the paper may serve as an effective marker. The slickness of the tape adds a tactile cue that is often more reinforcing than simply drawing a margin line. Students who have difficulty placing long or short letters on the appropriate line may benefit from having the lines highlighted with a colored marker. Students with severe difficulty in this skill may benefit from using a cardboard frame that forces the pencil to stop when it hits either the top or bottom line.

> Use of multi-sensory (visual-auditory-kinesthetic-tactile) strategies may be most helpful in teaching children the correct letter formations.

Students with spatial confusion often have particular difficulty organizing their work in math. Graph paper may help to teach them how to organize work simultaneously in horizontal and vertical planes.

Students with visual perception problems frequently reverse letters beyond the developmentally appropriate age. It is common for children to have more difficulty *drawing* letters in the correct orientation than *recognizing* letters that have been reversed or inverted. Use of multi-sensory (visual-auditory-kinesthetic-tactile) strategies may be most helpful in teaching children the correct letter formations.

Outside the Classroom

While many of the suggestions presented here can be readily incorporated into the classroom routine, others require the student to spend a considerable amount of time in supervised practice of specific skills.

Parents or other family members should be encouraged to supervise students in practice outside the school environment and to include assignments in motivating nonacademic formats. Examples might include copying the weekly grocery list from a parent's dictation or scanning the television guide to select and write a schedule of programs to watch during the week.

References

Benbow, M. (1988). *Loops and other groups: A kinesthetic writing system.* Randolph, NJ: O.T. Ideas.

Oliver, C.E. (1989). A sensorimotor program for improving writing readiness skills in elementary-age children. *American Journal of Occupational Therapy, 44*(2), 111-116.

PEANUTS

PEANUTS reprinted by permission of United Feature Syndicate, Inc.

Helping Hands: A World of Manipulatives to Boost Handwriting Skills

June M. Naus

To facilitate the appropriate development of handwriting skills, teachers should understand causes of writing problems and be aware of techniques that may be helpful in alleviating a child's frustration.

There is no substitute for the keen eyes of a teacher—and the ability to do something about what you see. Does Sarah, age 6, still hold her crayon in her fist? Does Richard, age 7, draw his letters with crabbed, cramped fingers? Does Tanya, age 10, still show no preference for either her left or her right hand? Does Hassad, age 8, intensely dislike writing? A teacher who notices these things and knows how to help can improve the educational prospects of such children.

The ability to write provides important advantages for a child. A child who can write well has improved confidence and self-esteem, increased concentration on content, improved academic performance, and the increased ability to express him- or herself creatively (Olsen, 1990). On the other hand, a child who has difficulty writing struggles with simple pencil-and-paper tasks and is likely to become discouraged when attempting to complete more demanding writing assignments. Yet, few elementary teachers have been trained to assist children with handwriting difficulties (Milone & Wasylyk, 1981). This unfortunate situation often causes both the teacher and the student to feel frustrated.

To facilitate the appropriate development of handwriting skills, teachers should understand causes of writing problems and be aware of techniques that may be helpful in alleviating a child's frustration. Recent research (Cornhill & Case-Smith, 1996) has found significant correlative and predictive relationships between a child's ability to perform in-hand manipulation tasks (the precise finger movements used in fine-motor tasks) and handwriting performance. This finding indicates that, as a child's ability to perform in-hand manipulation tasks improves, his or her handwriting skills will also improve.

This article identifies possible causes of handwriting difficulties and suggests activities to facilitate the development of hand muscles and handwriting skills. Although I have not addressed specific curriculums and techniques for teaching handwriting...I have provided general guide-lines for successfully teaching handwriting in the early childhood and primary elementary classrooms. Areas covered in this article include hand-writing readiness, wrist stability, hand development activities, pencil grasp, hand dominance, eye-hand coordination, basic strokes, general readiness skills, writing materials, and general classroom accommodations.

Handwriting Readiness

The hand development necessary for handwriting begins during infancy. As a young child reaches, points, grasps, and releases objects, the hand muscles strengthen; and the child develops the ability to make increas-ingly refined hand and finger movements. Eventually, the child is able to perform precise and skilled fine motor responses necessary for handwriting. Children who are pushed into handwriting before acquiring these or other necessary skills may become frustrated and discouraged, develop poor writing habits that are difficult to correct, and experience failure (Wright & Allen, 1975)....

Wrist Stability

In addition, performing the precise and skilled hand movements necessary for handwriting requires that the wrist be stabilized. This means that a child's wrist needs to be straight or slightly extended to provide maximum support for the hand during handwriting activities. Poor wrist posture, as evidenced by a bent wrist when drawing or writing, can be improved by having the child work in a vertical orientation, such as on a slant board, easel, blackboard, or felt board. The vertical orientation straightens the wrist and increases the child's hand and fine motor function. You can easily adapt drawing, writing, and other activities, as listed in Table 1, so that they are performed in a vertical orientation. Switching working surfaces from a horizontal to a vertical plane transforms many activities into powerful exercises for developing fine motor skills (Myers, 1992).

TABLE I. Increasing wrist stability

Activities to Do in a Vertical Orientation	
✔ Drawing and writing	✔ Painting
✔ Coloring	✔ Making pictures with stickers
✔ Telling flannel board stories	✔ Using geoboards or pegboards
✔ Using felt or magnetic letters, numbers, or manipulatives to complete tasks	

How can we meet students' individual needs in handwriting?

Hand Muscle Development

A straight wrist posture is necessary to provide appropriate support for the hands while writing and performing activities that require in-hand manipulation skills. *In-hand manipulation skills* are the precise and skilled finger movements made during fine motor tasks. Practice and refinement of tasks requiring in-hand manipulation help the child to develop the strength and coordination necessary to grasp, manipulate, and control writing instruments while writing. You can design in-hand manipulation tasks to enable the child to successfully participate in enjoyable classroom activities while developing the fine motor skills necessary for handwriting. ...early childhood and early elementary curriculums provide numerous opportunities to facilitate the development of small hand muscles and in-hand manipulation skills while achieving curricular objectives.

Arts and Crafts

In-hand manipulation skills are naturally a part of many arts and crafts activities. Students can make tissue paper pictures by tearing and rolling tissue paper into small balls and then gluing the balls to construction paper to create a design. Children can cut paper or felt into small pieces to make mosaics. In addition, students can make textured pictures by holding chalk or crayons sideways with the four fingers opposed to the thumb to draw or make imprints of items underneath the paper.

Mathematics

Mathematics offers a variety of opportunities to match, sort, and sequence small objects such as coins, buttons, and poker chips during mathematics. In addition, the child can cup and roll dice to create mathematical equations or play number games. Children can also roll play dough into tiny balls and use them as manipulatives to help solve equations. Finally, math facts bingo provides repeated opportunities to manipulate bingo chips.

Integrated Language Arts

During integrated language arts, children can use fine motor skills to illustrate stories by using crayons, markers, pencils, chalk, or a felt board and felt pieces (on a vertical surface is ideal). In addition, children can use wax-coated string, play dough, or clay to form letters. Teachers can color-code computer keyboards to encourage students to use specific fingers to press designated keys while typing letters, words, or sentences. Finally, you can glue small manipulatives to the letter that identifies their initial sounds (e.g., "Popcorn" can be glued to a large **P**).

Centers

Children can use more individualized materials during centers. The game *Magna Doodle* is ideal for drawing pictures and for copying or tracing letters. *Lite Brite* requires use of in-hand manipulation skills to pick up and plug in each peg. In addition, a child can shape, pinch, and search for items in clay or Theraputty (a nonhardening clay-like material that is available in five color-coded resistance levels ranging from soft to firm) or line up dominoes on their narrow ends. After the teacher has labeled clothespins with numbers or letters, the child can pinch the clothespins and clasp them to match letters, numbers, or answers to problems written on cardboard or paper.

Social Skill Development or Free Play

Many games and toys that provide opportunities for social interaction also increase hand muscle development. Dressing dolls and playing with miniature cars and games, such as *Don't Spill the Beans* and *Kerplunk,* are fun options. Another activity is to have the child squirrel objects into the hand with the thumb while continuing to hold the accumulated items, such as when children pick up jacks or other small game objects (Benbow, 1993).

A student can also develop hand muscles while assisting with classroom chores. Some tasks include stapling paper, punching holes with a hand-held punch, and wringing out sponges for cleaning desks and blackboards (Levine, 1991). Practicing activities in each of these curricular areas will facilitate hand development and, consequently, will help the child develop the in-hand manipulation skills necessary to grasp and manipulate writing instruments for handwriting.

Appropriate Pencil Grasp

As a child's hand muscles strengthen, he or she naturally develops increasingly effective pencil grasps. Initially, hand strength is devoted to stabilizing the writing instrument, and the child is able to make only random, uncontrolled marks. As the child's hands strengthen, however, his or her grasp transforms to increase control and to refine movements of the writing instrument for handwriting.

The most effective grasp is typically the *dynamic tripod grasp....* In this grip, the thumb and index finger form an open web space, working in opposition to each other to provide the greatest capacity for speed, flexibility, and refinement of hand movements.

Failure to maintain an open web space when holding a writing instrument indicates that the child's small hand muscles are lacking strength to maintain this grasp. Consequently, the activities...that facilitate hand muscle development are appropriate. If adequate strength is present, it is possible to force the "pinch" grasp by having the child write with small pieces of crayon or chalk. Forcing the child to hold the writing instrument with the pads of the thumb and fingers naturally maintains the open web space....

> **As a child's hand muscles strengthen, he or she naturally develops increasingly effective pencil grasps.**

Hand Dominance

As the hands strengthen, hand dominance also develops to facilitate efficient use of the hands. The dominant hand begins to develop skill and precision to perform fine motor tasks, such as writing and cutting, while the other hand supports and assists the action of the dominant hand. If hand dominance fails to emerge, neither hand acquires the refinement of skill that usually develops in the dominant hand with practice. This inadequacy makes handwriting very difficult.

Failure to reach past the midline of the body to grasp items or to draw is an indication that hand dominance is absent; often, a child without hand dominance will draw with the hand that is holding a writing instrument, displaying no preference to use either hand. Having the child sequence items with one hand can encourage reaching past the midline. In addition, playing "Simon Says" can motivate a child to reach across the center line of the body (e.g., "Simon" models touching the left foot with the right hand). Finally, Table 2 identifies several additional activities, such as cutting with scissors and drawing with stencils, that encourage the skill and support functions of the hands (Levine, 1991).

TABLE 2.

Writing Prerequisite	Activities*
Pencil Grasp	Small pieces of crayon or chalk Preschool crayons Pencil grip Primary-sized markers (with reminders to keep the tips of the fingers on the stripes)
Hand Dominance	Playing "Simon Says" Having the child sequence items with one hand Cutting with scissors Drawing with stencils, templates, or rulers Using a rotary pencil sharpener or egg beater Opening containers with lids Using wind-up toys Wearing a bracelet or ring as a reminder
Eye-Hand Coordination	Performing fingerplays . Lacing cards Stringing beads Playing with *Legos, Tinker Toys, Lite Brite, Lincoln Logs,* or snap beads Dressing dolls and playing with doll houses or miniature cars Playing *Barrel of Monkeys, Pic up Sticks, Cootie Bug, Operation, Don't Spill the Beans,* or *Don't Break the Ice* Completing puzzles Typing on a color-coded computer keyboard Drawing, tracing, coloring, or painting Completing dot-to-dot pictures Cutting
Basic Strokes	Filling in the missing parts of pictures and letters Tracing, copying, or drawing Completing dot-to-dot pictures Using stencils Air-writing Drawing lines to connect matching pictures Sand or water play Finger painting

* Activities designated to develop hand muscles will facilitate development of these prerequisites.

Eye-Hand Coordination

As the hands work together to perform a fine motor task, such as handwriting, the eyes provide pertinent information to guide hand and finger movements; few people can write neatly on lined paper without seeing the lines. This working relationship between the eyes and the hands is what is referred to as eye-hand coordination.

Eye-hand coordination depends on hand muscle development; small muscle control enables the hand to accomplish what the eye desires to see. Several activities (see Table 2) can help develop hand muscles, as well as eye-hand coordination; these activities require the child to respond to what he or she sees to precisely manipulate and position items. Some fun activities include lacing cards, stringing beads, playing with Legos™, and building with Lincoln Logs™. In addition, typing on a computer requires precise placement of the fingers, especially if the keys are color-coded to indicate which fingers need to press specific keys. Finally, paper-oriented tasks, such as drawing, tracing, cutting, and completing dot-to-dot pictures, are other fun ways to aid in the development of visual-motor skills (Lamme, 1979).

Basic Strokes

As the child's pencil grasp and eye-hand coordination develop, he or she begins to use these skills to scribble. Gradually, scribbling includes the use of basic strokes to form definite shapes and pictures. The basic strokes include vertical, horizontal, and diagonal lines, as well as circles and partial circle strokes (i.e., |, —, \, /, O, and C). To be prepared for handwriting instruction, the child should be able to draw these strokes smoothly and somewhat precisely. In addition, it is important that the child learn to make these strokes from top-to-bottom and from left-to-right (Wright & Allen, 1975).

Teachers can often evaluate a child's ability to make basic strokes by watching the child draw a picture. By examining a child's drawing of a person or a car, you can observe not only if the child is able to form lines and circles, but also how smoothly the strokes are drawn and how precisely the lines and circles are connected. Table 2 shows several other activities that encourage the formation of basic strokes. Some of these exercises include filling in the missing parts of pictures and letters, connecting dots, tracing, and drawing a line to connect matching pictures on paper or a blackboard.

General Readiness Skills

In addition to demonstrating the appropriate motor abilities for handwriting, children should display readiness skills in other developmental areas that are important for successful handwriting instruction. These skills include letter perception; orientation to printed language; interest in writing; following auditory, visual, or signed directions; and the ability to attend for a minimum of 1 minute.

Letter Perception

The child needs to have the ability to recognize forms and to distinguish and explain similarities and differences among them. Visual discrimination skills necessary for letter perception can be developed through use of activities that require matching, finding differences, and locating missing parts. Parquetry shapes, puzzles, and sorting also facilitate these skills.

Orientation to Printed Language

Activities that foster left-to-right directionality also help to stimulate interest in writing. Purposeful activities that expose children to the directionality of print include reading to them, labeling items in the classroom, writing stories as children dictate, following recipes, and having children "read" favorite rhymes and stories as a group.

Interest in Writing

In addition to the activities listed in the previous section, interest in writing is stimulated by providing activities that use handwriting for personal purposes, such as in making books, cards, maps, charts, signs, and letters to mail (Lamme, 1979).

Following Auditory, Visual, or Signed Directions

Following directions is necessary and inherent in almost all aspects of formal education. As a result, classroom routines, as well as games like "Simon Says" and copying lines (drawn one at a time) to ultimately create pictures, can provide practice.

The Ability to Attend for a Minimum of I Minute

Focused attention is necessary to complete most tasks. Stimulating interest and providing opportunities for success are key factors in maintaining a child's attention.

How can we meet students' individual needs in handwriting?

Writing Materials

What are appropriate materials to use when you begin instruction in handwriting? Research has found that choice of writing tools is unrelated to successful handwriting performance; as a result, children are encouraged to use the writing instruments that are most comfortable and motivating to them (Carlson & Cunningham, 1990; Lamme & Ayris, 1983). In addition, Lamme (1979) recommends using unlined paper until the child is able to write letters of consistent height. When lined paper is introduced, the width between the lines generally seems to depend on the age and skill of the child (Hill, Gladden, Porter, & Cooper, 1982). When using any lined paper, be sure the child can easily see the lines (Milone & Wasylyk, 1981).

General Classroom Accommodations

Teachers should be aware that classroom procedures can also influence the effectiveness of handwriting instruction or remediation. Here are some guidelines to increase success:

- Communicate the importance of handwriting.
- Teach handwriting directly in a highly structured lesson of no longer than 15 minutes.
- Use clear, consistent language to describe the formation of the strokes.
- Insist on good posture. (The child should sit upright, with the lower back against the back of the seat and elbows slightly off of the edge of the desk.)
- Check to see that the student's feet and desk rest firmly on the floor.
- Make sure that the paper is positioned at 20-35 degrees to the left for right-handers and 30-35 degrees to the right for left-handers. (Put tape on the desk to help the student align the paper.)
- Display models of good writing.
- Emphasize a preference for high-quality work instead of large quantities of sloppy writing.
- Set criteria for acceptable work, and teach the children to evaluate their own writing.
- Return unacceptable work to the student until he or she meets the criteria, especially at the beginning of the year.

- Provide immediate feedback when possible (Milone & Wasylyk, 1981; Hofmeister, 1973).

In addition, teachers can make some basic accommodations in the classroom to compensate for inadequacies in handwriting. Here are several suggestions (Levine, 1987):

- Although being understanding of the student's problem, hold him or her accountable for working to full potential.

- Modify requirements based on how quickly a student's penmanship begins to deteriorate.

- Set realistic goals for the amount of time a student needs to complete an assignment.

- Make accommodations to prevent difficulties with handwriting from interfering with performance in all academic areas (e.g., using short-answer or circled responses).

- Break writing tasks into simple components to be completed in steps.

- Provide positive feedback for effort by giving two grades to evaluate content and legibility.

- Give the student a copy of criteria to conduct self-evaluations.

These suggestions may help to improve the performances and attitudes of students with handwriting difficulties.

Final Thoughts

Teachers who are informed about handwriting difficulties and prewriting skills can assist their students in many ways. Of course, teachers should consider the individual abilities and interests of each student when implementing these, or any other, interventions. Using activities that are appropriate and motivating for each student is critical in facilitating successful handwriting.

References ─────────────

Benbow, M. (1993, January). Parent-teacher activities to develop hand skills in young children. Paper presented at the Development of Hand Skills conference at Towson State University, Towson, MD.

Carlson, K., & Cunningham, J. (1990). Effect of pencil diameter on the graphomotor skill of preschoolers. *Early Childhood Research Quarterly, 5*, 279-293.

Cornhill, H., & Case-Smith, J. (1996). Factors that relate to good and poor handwriting. *American Journal of Occupational Therapy, 50*, 732-739.

Hill, D. S., & Gladden, M. A., Porter, J. T., & Cooper, J. O. (1982). Variables affecting transition from wide-spaced to normal-spaced paper for manuscript handwriting. *Journal of Educational Research, 76,* 50-53.

Hofmeister, A. M. (1973). Let's get it write. *Teaching Exceptional Children, 6*(1), 30-33.

Lamme, L. (1979). Handwriting in an early childhood curriculum. *Young Children, 35*(1), 20-27.

Lamme, L. L., & Ayris, B. M. (1983). Is the handwriting of beginning writers influenced by writing tools? *Journal of Research and Development in Education, 17,* 32-38.

Levine, K. J. (1991). *Fine motor dysfunction: Therapeutic strategies for the classroom.* Tucson, AZ: Therapy Skill Builders.

Levine, M. (1987). *Developmental variation and learning disorders.* Cambridge, MA: Educational Publishing Service.

Milone, M. N., & Wasylyk, T. M. (1981). Handwriting in special education. *Teaching Exceptional Children, 14*(2), 58-61.

Myers, C. A. (1992). Therapeutic fine-motor activities for preschoolers. In J. Case-Smith, & C. Pehoski (Eds.), *Development of hand skills in the child* (pp. 47-62). Rockville, MD: American Occupational Therapy Association.

Olsen, J. (1990). *Handwriting without tears.* Brookfield, IL: Fred Sammons.

Wright, J. P., & Allen, E. G. (1975). Ready to write. *Elementary School Journal, 75,* 430-435.

"I'm not gonna have room on this postcard to tell them much."

Reprinted with special permission of King Features Syndicate.

Teaching the Left-Handed Writer

Clinton S. Hackney and William Hendricks

In the average classroom, there are two to four "lefties" who have special needs that must be considered by the teacher.

Approximately ten percent of all people are left-handed. This often-overlooked minority includes many famous and gifted people, such as Bill Clinton, Prince Charles, Norman Schwarzkopf, Oprah Winfrey, Benjamin Franklin, and Henry Ford. In the average classroom, there are two to four "lefties" who have special needs that must be considered by the teacher. Yet many right-handed teachers are unaware of the subtle ways in which classroom tools and activities can be biased. Pencil sharpeners face the wrong way, notebook spirals dig into the hand, the cutting edge of scissors is upside down, and tight seating at tables causes elbows to bump. Right-handed teachers may practice the left-handed position themselves to better understand the needs of left-handed writers.

Determining Hand Dominance

Early childhood teachers may encounter children who have not yet developed a clear preference for one hand or the other. If the child is definitely left-handed, it is better to teach him or her to use that hand in writing. If, however, there is some doubt as to which is the dominant hand, there are several simple ways of determining which will be the hand to train. Working with one child at a time, observe the student in the following situations. Be careful to let the child pick up the testing materials; do not hand them to the child. Keep a record of the results; if a child is truly ambidextrous, it is probably better to train the right hand.

Hand puppet—Place a puppet on the table and observe which hand the child puts the puppet on.

...many right-handed teachers are unaware of the subtle ways in which classroom tools and activities can be biased.

Key and lock—Padlock a cupboard and place the key on a table. Ask the child to take the key, unlock the padlock, and bring you an object from the cupboard. Observe hand preference.

Hammering nails—Observe the child's hand preference as he or she hammers pegs with a toy hammer or places pegs in a pegboard.

Screwing lids on jars—Place several jars of different sizes in one pile and the matching lids in another. Observe handedness as the child matches the lids to the jars.

Throwing a ball—On the playground, ask the child to pick up a ball and throw it to you.

Discouraging the "Hooked" Writing Position

Handwriting can be an especially difficult area for left-handers. Without good instruction, left-handers may develop bad writing habits, including the tendency to "hook" the wrist in order to see what they are writing. Emphasize the correct pencil and paper positions for left-handed writers, shown below, to help students develop good habits.

Paper Position for Left-Handed Writers

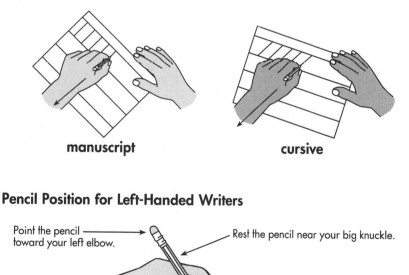

manuscript   cursive

Pencil Position for Left-Handed Writers

Point the pencil toward your left elbow.

Rest the pencil near your big knuckle.

Hold the pencil with your first two fingers and thumb.

Bend your thumb.

Rest your last two fingers on the paper.

Hints for Handwriting

Although teachers may find that left-handed students in their class-rooms have already developed awkward handwriting, it is not necessary to lower expectations for these students. The suggestions that follow will help left-handed students write as well as right-handed students.

- Emphasize correct paper position to help left-handed writers resist twisting or "hooking" their hands and wrists in order to see what they are writing.

- Make available the Zaner-Bloser Writing Frame, or pencil grips specially made for left-handers, to help students position their hands and hold their pencils correctly.

- Suggest that left-handed students hold their pencils slightly farther back than right-handed students. This allows them to see what they are writing.

- Seat left-handed writers to the left of the chalkboard for better visibility.

- Encourage left-handed writers to practice writing at the chalk-board for full, free arm movement.

- Occasionally, group left-handed students together for handwriting instruction.

- If table and arm chairs are used, make sure left-handed students are not seated at desks designed for right-handed students.

- If possible, provide left-handed scissors and other left-handed tools.

- Be aware that reversing letters is a common problem for the left-handed child. Most errors result from confusion between manu-script **d** and **b** and **p** and **q**. To help, concentrate on formally teaching left-to-right progression and the correct formation of forward and backward circles before introducing these letters.

Teachers should be aware of the left-handers in their classrooms and plan support for them. Care should be taken, however, to avoid attention that will make left-handers self-conscious. Showing sensitivity to the needs of these students can build self-esteem and make left-handers a bit more comfortable in a "right-handed world."

How can we meet students' individual needs in handwriting?